NEW YORK: OLD AND NEW

SECOND EDITION

OLD HOUSE, SIXTY-FIRST STREET AND EAST RIVER, KNOWN AS SMITH'S FOLLY

New York: Old & New

Its Story, Streets, and Landmarks

BY RUFUS ROCKWELL WILSON

AUTHOR OF "WASHINGTON: THE CAPITAL CITY," "RAMBLES IN COLONIAL BYWAYS," ETC.

WITH MANY ILLUSTRATIONS FROM PRINTS AND PHOTOGRAPHS

AND WITH DECORATIONS BY EDWARD STRATTON HOLLOWAY

VOL. II

PHILADELPHIA & LONDON

J. B. LIPPINCOTT COMPANY

1903

Published October, 1902

Electrotyped and Printed by
J. B. Lippincott Company, Philadelphia, U. S. A.

CONTENTS

VOL. II

Section One—*Through the Old City*

Section Two—*The Common to Love Lane*

CONTENTS

Section Three—*Bloomingdale and Beyond*

ILLUSTRATIONS

VOL. II

ILLUSTRATIONS

SECTION ONE

THROUGH THE OLD CITY

I

Bowling Green & Battery

OLD New York lies buried beneath the tidal-wave of its own material prosperity. The man born and bred therein, returning after long absence, finds it so changed that for him the town he knew in his youth has become a thing of dreams. While growth and additions work the principal changes in other cities, New York "not only adds to itself, but incessantly rends itself in pieces;" and this work of levelling and rearing anew goes on without ceasing in all parts of the town. Wall Street within the memory of living men has been thrice rebuilt, and the same is true of Broadway, the Bowery, and Fifth Avenue. The New York of fifty, nay thirty, years ago, although a great city, survives only in the course of its principal streets and in a few public buildings and churches.

And yet, for those who can discern it, old New York still lives and has a being,—a city charged with romance and suggestion and with paves echoing the foot-falls of men whose memory the world will not let die. Every nook and corner in the older quarters of the town, rich in its associations with by-gone times, is sacred ground to the man who loves the past. The pages that follow record many pilgrimages to these memory-haunted places and thoroughfares, and if now and then they carry the reader beyond the boundaries of the ancient town, rich gleanings in mellowed fields shall be their excuse and his most abundant reward.

Let the first of these pilgrimages begin where the town began,—at and around the Bowling Green, the name given to the bit of ground at the southern end of Broadway which has never been diverted from public use since the foundation of the city. When Fort Amsterdam was built, in the day of first things, the open space opposite its northern wall and sally-port was set apart for common use, and soon became the most frequented quarter of the town. Here centred its social life; here the children of the little hamlet played on summer afternoons; and here youths and maidens danced on holidays, and on the first of each returning May, with much innocent rejoicing, crowned their loveliest with flowers. The Plain, as it was called before it became known as the Bowling Green, was also the parade-ground for the soldiers, and here, too, were held the annual fairs, the one for cattle and the other for hogs, instituted by Director Kieft, who, we are told, materially added to the number of visitors by decreeing that no one should be arrested for debt during their continuance.

When the rule of the Dutch gave way to that of the English, the plain before the fort continued to be used for public purposes, and in March, 1732, we find the city fathers resolving "that this corporation will lease a piece of land lying at the lower end of Broadway, fronting to the Fort, to some of the inhabitants of said Broadway, in order to be enclosed to make a Bowling Green thereof, with walks therein, for the beauty and ornament of said street, as well as for the recreation and delight of the inhabitants of the city." John Chambers, Peter

Bayard, and Peter Jay thus became lessees of the Bowling Green at an annual rental of one pepper-corn, and when this lease expired it was renewed for another eleven years on payment of twenty shillings per annum. We are not told how long the Green continued to be devoted to the sport of bowls, but it comes again into view in August, 1770, when it was made to furnish a site for an equestrian statue of George III., set up by the provincial assembly as a token of popular gratitude for the repeal of the Stamp Act. The following year it was ordered: "Whereas the General Assembly of this Province have been at the great expense of sending for an equestrian statue of his present majesty and erected the same on the Bowling Green, before his majesty's fort in this city, and this Board conceiving that unless the Green be fenced in the same will very soon become a receptacle for all the filth and dirt in the neighborhood, in order to prevent which it is ordered that the same be fenced with iron rails, with a stone foundation, at an expense of eight hundred pounds." The stones and fence then put in place still surround the Green, shorn, however, of the crowns which originally ornamented the tops of the pillars.

Bowling Green's part in the Revolution and

the sorry though not unfitting fate which overtook the statue of the king—it was of lead mounted on a granite pedestal—have been dealt with in another place. Following the conclusion of peace, use of the Green was in 1786 granted for two years to Chancellor Livingston, on condition that he should, "at his own expense, manure the ground, and sow the same with grass seed, and have it well laid down as a green;" but this arrangement came soon to an end, and in 1795 it was ordered "that the enclosed ground, commonly called the Bowling Green, be appropriated to the use of the governor for the time being." The governor, however, made only brief use of this privilege, and in 1798 it was ordered "that Mr. John Rogers may have the use of the Bowling Green, on condition that he keep it in good order, and suffer no creatures to run in it." Before this it had assumed its present shape; and the opening of a new century found it—the tenancy of Rogers having also terminated—relegated to municipal care and on the way to become, what it has since remained, a little sister to the Battery.

The Battery, as its name implies, was in the early days ostensibly devoted to warlike purposes. The easy taking of Fort Amsterdam in

1664 proved the importance of so strengthening that defence that it could be held by its new masters should the Dutch, as seemed more than probable, attempt its recapture. "The Fort," Stuyvesant wrote in explaining its surrender, "is situated in an untenable place, where it was located on the first discovery of New Netherland, for the purpose of resisting an attack of the barbarians rather than an assault of European arms; having, within pistol shot on the north and southeast sides, higher ground than that on which it stands, so that, notwithstanding the walls and works are raised highest on that side, people standing and walking on that high ground can see the soles of the feet of those on the esplanades and bastions of the fort." The English at once set to work to remedy these defects, and the raising of the walls of the fort having been put aside as impracticable, it was finally decided to build a supporting battery under its walls. Thus in due time five demiculverins were put in place on the rocks below the fort. These gave way in 1689 to "a half-moon mounting seven great guns," and four years later it was decided to build "a battery of fifty guns on the outside point of rocks under the fort, so situated as to command both rivers." More than a generation was required to transform this decision into action. Ratzen's map of 1767, however, shows the Battery as completed, and we know that during the Revolution a line of works extended from the foot of Greenwich Street along the water-front to Whitehall Slip.

The fort which had borne so many names was demolished in 1790 to furnish a site, first for the Government House, then for a row of dwellings, and finally for a custom-house. The Battery at the same time fell into disuse and decay; but was built up anew during the second war with England. Meanwhile, what was known as the Southwest Battery had been erected on a ledge a hundred yards or so from the shore, access to which was by means of a long bridge with a draw. This at a later time was called Castle Clinton, but its six-foot walls armed with twenty-eight thirty-two-pounders never felt the blows of an enemy, and when, in 1822, the federal government took possession of Governor's Island, it was ceded to the city, whereupon the ground included between Castle Clinton and the former Battery—a crescent-shaped piece of ground of about ten acres, since doubled in size by filling in—was made into a park, while Castle Clinton, passing by lease into private hands, was converted into a public assembly-room and renamed Castle Garden.

The old fort became immediately a place of fashionable resort, and for a long time its rows of wooden benches were thronged on summer evenings by the quality of the town. There Lafayette landed on his return to America in 1824, " on a carpeted stairway arranged for the occasion, under an arch richly decorated with flags and wreaths of laurel." The same evening, runs a contemporary chronicle, an immense balloon arose from the old fort, " representing the famous horse Eclipse mounted by an ancient knight in armor." When, a few weeks later, the nation's guest returned from a tour of other cities, " a splendid *fête* and gala was given to him at Castle Garden, which for grandeur, expense and entire effect was never before witnessed in this country. About six thousand persons were assembled in that immense area, and, the evening being clear and calm, the whole passed off happily, owing to the excellent arrangements of the committee."

Clay and Webster spoke more than once in Castle Garden, and there receptions were given to Jackson and many another President. There also the elders of the city welcomed Louis Kossuth, when in 1851 he came to America to seek aid for Hungary, and thence he was escorted to his hotel by a procession long remembered for its size and enthusiasm. His was undeniably the most magnificent reception ever tendered a foreigner in this country, excepting only Lafayette; and the famous Hungarian was worthy of all the honors heaped upon him. He remained in New York for several weeks, speaking almost every evening to large meetings of different nationalities, always on an appropriate theme and in their mother-tongue, and by his oratory and his picturesqueness making captive each new audience. He failed, nevertheless, in the main object of his visit,—to procure American intervention in the affairs of his native country,—and we respect him the more that in his after years he discreetly resented our noisy but barren sympathy.

Castle Garden during this period was also the occasional home of grand opera. "The city of New York is so overgrown," wrote Philip Hone, in May, 1845, "that we in the upper regions do not know much more of what is passing in the lower, nor the things which are to be seen there, than the inhabitants of Mexico or Grand Cairo. I was informed by a notice which I saw accidentally in a newspaper that the Italian opera company was to perform on Friday evening at Castle Garden. When I entered I found myself on the floor of the most splendid and the largest theatre I ever saw,—a place capable of seating comfortably six or eight thousand persons. The pit or pavilion is provided with some hundreds of small white tables and movable chairs, by which people are enabled to congregate in little squads and take their ices between the acts. In front of the stage is a beautiful fountain, which plays when the performers do not. The whole of this large area is surmounted by circular benches above and below, from every point of which the view is enchanting." He then enumerates the members of the company, and adds, "All this, and plenty of fresh air, if the weather should be ever warm enough to require it, for the moderate price of fifty cents."

Jenny Lind sang for the first time in America on September 11, 1850, under the management of Phineas T. Barnum. That clever showman had skilfully advertised her coming, and at her first concert in Castle Garden a great multitude gave her eager and joyous welcome. Their enthusiasm had generous reward, for Jenny Lind was perhaps the greatest singer of a generation that numbered many great singers. An aria or a folk-song phrased by her revealed beauties of which nobody had dreamed, and, when she chose to use it, there was a pathetic quality in her voice, a soprano of great richness, volume, and power, that vibrated in the feeling even to tears. To hear her sing "Home, Sweet Home" was to weep, while so sincere was her reverence for her art that she always inspired even those who knew little of music with much of her own ardor and emotion. Thus her successive concert tours in America—before she crossed the Atlantic she had abjured the stage—became a series of triumphal marches. Town and countryside raved about her; and wherever she sang every roof and window for blocks from the concert-hall was packed with people waiting to see her pass. Once when she dropped her shawl from a balcony, it was caught and in a moment torn into shreds by the eager crowd below. The material fruits of this enthusiasm were abundant. She gave a hundred and fifty concerts in America, thirty-five of them scarcely satisfying New York's craving for the Swedish idol; and so generous were the receipts that after giving away more than half of her share in charity, she carried back to Europe an ample fortune, the income from which sufficed to support her in comfort during thirty-six years of honored and delightful retirement.

After Jenny Lind came Mario and Grisi, then the most widely known members of the guild of singers, who on September 4, 1854, made their first appearance in America at Castle Garden. Grisi when she came to this country was as a vocalist no longer young, but as an actress she was still brilliant, powerful, and impetuous, and by her intensity and fire proved herself a supreme mistress of dramatic art. Mario, on the other hand, was in his prime both of voice and person, the prince of romance singers and easily the sweetest tenor America has ever heard. With Mario and Grisi came Signor Susini, a noble basso who looked the soldier he had been in his youth, and Signorina Vestvali, who by her fresh contralto voice, handsome face, and stately presence thrilled the town for a day and then disappeared to be heard of no more.

Castle Garden's days as a home of opera came to an end in 1854, when the Academy of Music was opened in Fourteenth Street. The following year it was leased by the State Board of Emigration, and made a landing-place for immigrants, serving that purpose until 1890, when the federal government took charge of immigration and transferred the offices to Ellis Island. During the thirty-five years that it served as a landing-station, nearly ten millions of immigrants passed through its portals and went forth to fill the land with sturdy men and women. It is still a magnet for many of those who first landed there, and who when opportunity offers never fail to revisit it. One such visitor not long ago was a man of substance from the West, who said to an attendant, though in no boastful spirit, that in such-and-such a year he had come ashore in that building with all his earthly possessions rolled up in a newspaper. "And now I could buy the building and the land it stands on," he added. "It would be worth a lot of money," suggested the attendant. "I've got it," was the reply. When Castle Garden ceased to be a landing-station it passed to the jurisdiction of the municipal department of public parks, and since December, 1896, it has been known and used as the New York Aquarium; but not before the hand of the restorer had once more made it as it was when used as a place of defence, and occupied by troops. It was found impracticable, however, to rebuild the walk at the top of the fort, torn down after a partial destruction by fire in 1876, while the stretch of water which as late as 1853 separated it from the shore is now buried under greensward.

In the days when Castle Garden was still a place of fashionable amusement the streets adjoining and fronting the Battery were the favorite abiding-place of wealth and fashion. "Long after the uptown movement began," Richard Grant White, writing from boyhood memories, tells us, "people who were already housed near the Battery, or who could afford to get houses there, lingered lovingly around it. And well they might do so, for a place of city residence more delightful or convenient could not be found. Within five or ten minutes' walk of Wall and South Streets, where the great merchants had their counting-houses, it was yet entirely removed from business; and its surroundings made mere living there a pleasure. State Street, the eastern boundary of the Battery, was unsurpassed, if it was ever equalled, as a place of town residence; for living there was living on a park with a grand water view. The prospect from the windows and balconies of the old State Street houses included the bay with its islands and the shore of New Jersey. In summer, the western breezes blew upon these windows straight from the water. The sight here on

OLD HOUSE IN STATE STREET, FACING THE BATTERY

spring and summer and autumn evenings, when splendid sunsets—common then, but rare now, because of changes in the surrounding country, which have affected the formation and disposition of the clouds—made the firmament and water blaze with gold and color, seemed sometimes in their gorgeousness almost to surpass the imagination. It was a matter of course that such a place should be chosen as the site of the homes of wealthy people. The houses were most of them very simple in their exterior; but they had an air of large and elegant domesticity which proved them the homes of people of taste and character."

And such they remained until Castle Garden became an immigrant station. Then they were quickly abandoned by their owners and given over to vile and vulgar uses. Between 1855 and 1890 no spot in New York was more depraved than that in the neighborhood of Castle Garden, with its cheap lodging-houses and its low groggeries, whose keepers flourished by waylaying and robbing the never-ending stream of immigrants. The removal of the station to Ellis Island, however, put an end to these sordid conditions, and during the last ten years State Street and Battery Place have become, what they promise to remain, a great office-building district. This is as it should be, for, since in 1898 New York greatly enlarged its borders, Bowling Green—with the new custom-house rising on the site of the ancient fort, and tall business structures springing up all around it—has become the geographical centre of the greater city.

During the later colonial period and until the middle years of the last century Battery Park or Battery Walk, as it was indifferently called, was the favorite promenade of the growing town; and more than one piquant memory clings to its walks and shaded places. There Talleyrand, lame and keen-eyed, unfrocked priest and restless intriguer, faced one of the supreme moments of an uncommon career. He had fled from France to England and then to this country, because the Jacobins, with Robespierre at their head, wished to bring him to the guillotine. "I remember," said he, in telling the story to his secretary, Bourdaleau, "upon one occasion having been gifted for a single instant with an unknown and nameless power. I know not to this moment whence it came; it has never once returned, and yet on that one occasion it saved my life. I had freighted a ship with Beaumetz. He was a good fellow, Beaumetz, with whom I had ever lived in perfect harmony. We had fled from France; we had arrived in New York together. So, having resolved to improve the little money left us by speculation, it was still in partnership that we freighted a small vessel for India, trusting to all the goodly chances which had befriended us in our escape from danger and death. Everything was in readiness for our departure; we were waiting for a fair wind with the most eager expectation, prepared to embark at any hour of the day or night in obedience to a warning from the captain. This state of uncertainty seemed to irritate the temper of Beaumetz, who one day entered our lodging evidently laboring under great excitement, although commanding himself to appear calm. I was engaged at the moment in writing letters to Europe. Looking over my shoulder, he said, with forced gayety, 'What need to waste time in penning letters? They will never reach their destination. Come with me and let us take a turn on the Battery; perhaps the wind may chop round; we may be nearer our departure than we imagine.' The day was fine, and I suffered myself to be persuaded. We walked through the crowded streets to the Battery, Beaumetz seizing my arm and hurrying me along. When we had arrived at the esplanade he quickened his step still more until we reached close to the water's edge. He talked loud and quickly, admiring, in energetic terms, the beauty of the scenery, the ships riding at anchor, and the busy scene on the peopled wharf. Suddenly he paused—for I had freed my arm from his grasp and stood immovable before him. Staying his wild and rapid steps I fixed my eye upon him. He turned aside cowed and dismayed. 'Beaumetz!' I shouted, 'you mean to murder me; you intend to throw me into the sea. Deny it, monster, if you can.' The maniac stared at me for a moment, but I took especial care not to avert my gaze from his countenance, and he quailed beneath it. He stammered a few incoherent words and strove to pass me, but I barred his passage with extended arms. He looked vacantly right and left and then flung himself upon my neck and burst into tears. ''Tis true, my friend, 'tis true!' he cried. 'The thought has haunted me day and night like a flash from the lurid fire of hell. It was for this I brought you. Look! You stand within a foot of the edge of the parapet; in another instant the work would have been done.' The demon had left him; his eye was unsettled and the white foam stood in bubbles on his parched lips, but he was no longer tossed by the same mad excitement under which he had been laboring; he suffered me to lead him home without a single word. A few days of bleeding, repose, and abstinence restored him to his former self, and, what is most extraordinary, the circumstance was never mentioned between us. My fate was at work."

More than one literary wraith walks o'nights in Battery Park, for its paves, which in other days often echoed the foot-falls of Howe and Clinton, of Arnold and André, of Washington and Jefferson, of Burr and Hamilton, of Jerome Bonaparte and Louis Philippe, have also known Irving, Cooper, Halleck, Drake, Willis, and Morris. This corner of Manhattan lives again in the "Knickerbocker's History of New York;" Taylor and Stedman have celebrated its charms in verse; Howells has given it a place in at least two of his novels; and Edgar Fawcett has laid one of the scenes of "A Romance of Old New York" in the Bowling Green. Other luminous memories, real and fancied, attach to the thoroughfares adjacent to and adjoining the Battery. A warehouse covers the site of the school in Beaver Street near Whitehall in which for several years Henry William Herbert, better remembered as Frank Forrester, was a teacher of languages, and in an upper room of the Stevens House, upon the opposite side of Broadway, he died by his own hand. The hero of Bunner's "The Story of a New York House" lived at No. 7 State Street, and five doors removed on the opposite side once resided Washington Irving's elder brother, William, the Pindar Cockloft of "Salmagundi;" while James K. Paulding long dwelt at the corner of Whitehall and Stone Streets.

Finally, it was in a lodging-house lately gone from near-by West Street that in the autumn of 1879 Robert Louis Stevenson spent his first night in America. The gifted Scotsman has partly described in "The Amateur Emigrant" the manner of his voyage to New York, and what befell him at his journey's end. Limited means, and a wish to husband them to the utmost, impelled him upon landing to seek quarters at the Reunion House at No. 10 West Street, and there he lodged until he set out for California. The humble hostelry has now given way to a warehouse, but it lives again in Stevenson's delightful pages, and adds another to the full sheaf of memories which attend upon a stroll around the Bowling Green and the Battery.

II

A Walk in Pearl Street

PEARL STREET is New York's oldest thoroughfare. Starting where Broadway, under the name of State Street, fronts Battery Park, it curves towards the east, and expanding like a river in pools, first at Hanover and then at Franklin Square, turns finally to the westward, and enters Broadway next above Duane Street. Time was when Pearl Street, known first as the Strand and later as Great Dock and as Queen Street, faced the river, so much have the waters of the harbor been encroached upon; and it was until long after the colonial period the most travelled thoroughfare in the town. Seventy years ago it was still a street of elegant residences and of fine shops, and, though now sadly fallen from its former estate, its every crook and corner is charged with piquant suggestion for the lover of olden days and ways.

If a stroll through Pearl Street has its beginning at the Battery, one finds in the block between State and Whitehall Streets the site of the church Wouter Van Twiller built for Domine Bogardus, and of the house in which John Howard Payne entered life. Payne's story is one of the romances of old New York. He was a boy prodigy on the stage, and a commonplace actor in his maturity. Thrown into a London jail for debt, he opened his prison door with a successful piece of play-making. Then he sent some plays in manuscript to Charles Kemble. One of these was " Clari, the Maid of Milan," now remembered only through the song for which it was the original setting,—" Home Sweet Home." That plaintive ballad, wedded to the melody the loitering playwright had first heard sung by an Italian peasant girl, melted the heart of London and of the world, and with its one touch of nature that makes the whole world kin rendered Payne's name immortal. Its author, however, never again wrote or did anything memorable. He returned to America, and in 1843 he was appointed consul at Tunis, where in 1852, " an exile from home," he died. Thirty years later his remains were brought back to his native land, and laid finally in Oak Hill Cemetery, near Washington. The federal city holds many monuments, but none of them is visited by a greater throng of pilgrims nor shrines a memory with a tenderer appeal to all of them than that of the "wide-wandering actor who lived and died alone, and of whom nothing is remembered but that he wrote one song."

Going a little farther afield, a turn southward into Whitehall brings one to the spot, midway between Pearl and Front Streets, where river and island met when the town was young, and where Stuyvesant built the house which Dongan renamed Whitehall. Thence eastward and southward stretched the basin that sheltered vessels whose captains paid the city for the privilege of harbor. Blocks of warehouses now hold down the buried waters, but visible reminders of the colonial period have not been wholly swept away from this quarter of the town, and on the southeast corner of Pearl and Broad Streets Fraunces's Tavern still gives welcome to the wayfarer after an unbroken existence as a house of entertainment of nearly one hundred and fifty years. This historic house, one of the oldest now standing on Manhattan Island, was built by Stephen De Lancey in the early part of the eighteenth century, and in 1750 Oliver De Lancey seems to have had his residence either here or in the adjoining house. Twelve years later the building was sold at auction, and purchased by

Samuel Fraunces, a West Indian, who opened a tavern under the sign of Queen Charlotte, which was for many years one of the most popular hostelries in the growing town.

Fraunces proved a stanch friend of the patriot cause when the Revolution came, and played a worthy, if modest, part in the stirring events of the time. He went out with the patriots in 1776, but appears later to have returned to the city, mayhap by British permission under arrangement with Washington, and to have resided here during at least a part of the British occupation, as his generous advances to the American prisoners at that time confined in the city afterwards prompted a vote of thanks and a handsome grant of money from Congress. It was in the Long Room of Fraunces's Tavern that, on November 25, 1783, at the close of the military movements attending the surrender of the city by the British, Governor George Clinton gave a dinner to the commander-in-chief and other general officers of the patriot forces; but the event by reason of which the old inn will always claim a place in our history occurred nine days later, when, on December 4, in this same Long Room, Washington took farewell of his generals before setting out for Annapolis to surrender his commission to Congress. Mine host Fraunces was not forgotten in the bestowal of rewards which followed the success of the patriot cause and the founding of the republic. When, in 1789, Washington returned to New York to be inaugurated President and took up his residence here, he made Fraunces steward of his household, a post for which the latter was admirably fitted and which he filled with satisfaction to all concerned; and so his humble name has a place in our annals side by side with that of his great patron.

Fraunces's Tavern was originally three stories in height, and tradition has it that it was built of brick brought from Golden's yard in Amsterdam. Fire visited the building in 1853, but did no serious damage. In the repairs made at that time the Dutch roof surmounting the house gave way to two additional flat-topped stories. The lower portion of the house retained its original shape until 1890, when the wall was taken down and replaced by a pretentious stone front, and the old tap-room, scene of so many merry gatherings in the vanished days, was converted into a modern bar-room. The hand of the innovator, however, stopped short of the Long Room on the second floor. This is an apartment forty-three feet in length and twenty in width. Its walls are hung with a picture of the old tavern, a time-stained copy of the Declaration of Independence, a portrait of Washington, and other silent yet eloquent tokens of the history and associations of the place. The laying of a new floor excepted, the Long Room has not changed since in 1768 the Chamber of Commerce was organized within its walls. The antique wall-cupboard holds its long accustomed place, and just across the narrow hall-way is the old kitchen, unchanged save by the introduction of a modern range. On the third floor are several small guest-rooms, rarely used at present, but which, except as to furniture, stand just as they did a century ago when their occupants could look down upon Coffee-House Slip and the Merchant's Exchange. The present generation has witnessed one well-remembered scene at Fraunces's Tavern,—the memorial lunch given by the members of the Chamber of Commerce in December, 1883, in honor of its institution in the Long Room, and the supper in the evening in commemoration of Washington's farewell to his officers, when the Society of the Sons of the Revolution was organized by John Austin Stevens. The room was then "decorated in the old style. A turtle feast was had,

COFFEE HOUSE SLIP AND NEW YORK COFFEE-HOUSE, 1856

—the service by men in ancient garb,—long pipes were smoked, and the toasts were drunk in tobies of ale to the accompaniment of a drum and fife played by musicians in Continental uniform, who marched around the tables to hurrahs for Washington."

It is but a few steps from Fraunces's Tavern to Coenties Slip and to No. 73 Pearl Street, the site of the ancient Stadt Huys, New York's first City Hall; and four doors removed, on the same side of the way, one comes upon the spot, marked by a tablet, where William Bradford, New York's first printer, had his press. This worthy man voyaged from England to Philadelphia in 1685, armed with a letter from George Fox which announced to the Quakers of the colonies that "a sober young man, whose name is William Bradford, is coming to set up the trade of printing Friends' books." Bradford started his press in Philadelphia, but soon quarelled with his fellow-Quakers as to what he should and should not print, and when they sent him to jail for disregarding their commands, he sought a more congenial field of labor in New York. Thus it was that in April, 1693, he transferred his press to Pearl Street, and became, by appointment of the council, public printer to the colony. Bradford continued for nearly fifty years a useful and hard-working citizen of New York. Besides fulfilling the duties of his office, he found time to print many books and pamphlets now dear to the heart of the collector; and in 1725 he founded the *New York Gazette,* the first and for several years the only newspaper in the town. He was also the master and trainer of an entire generation of printers, including John Peter Zenger, whose brave fight for a free press was acclaimed by Gouverneur Morris "the morning star of that liberty that subsequently revolutionized America." Bradford died in 1752, at the age of ninety, and the stone above his grave in Trinity burial-ground tells the wayfarer that "he was printer to this government for upward of fifty years, and being quite worn out with old age and labor he left this mortal state in lively hopes of a blessed immortality."

Pearl Street at Old Slip opens out into Hanover Square, formerly a favorite residence section, and the great shopping centre of fashion during the colonial and Revolutionary periods. Here the Cotton Exchange covers the site of the building from which Bradford issued his *New York Gazette;* and close at hand, at the vanished sign of the Bible and Crown, another famous pioneer printer plied his craft for nearly half a century. This was the Irishman, Hugh Gaine, an interesting if not heroic figure in the times that tried men's souls. Gaine appeared in New York in 1745 and seven years later began his *New York Mercury*. This newspaper was originally edited in the interest of the Whigs, but when the Revolution came and the British occupied New York, Gaine's prudence got the better of his convictions,—if he had any,—and he became a stanch advocate of the royalist cause. The war ended, true to his shifty nature, he petitioned the assembly to allow him to remain in the city and to continue his paper. The petition was granted, but the *Mercury* no longer found favor with its readers, and in November, 1783, its existence came to an end. Thereafter Gaine devoted himself to general printing, and among the steady stream of pamphlets, almanacs, and books that poured from his press was the first American edition of "Robinson Crusoe." He died in 1807, at the age of eighty-one, and lies buried in Trinity church-yard.

Four years after Gaine's death Hanover Square became the abiding-place of the famous French general Victor Moreau, banished from France on a charge of conspiracy to assassinate

Napoleon. Moreau took up his residence at No. 119 Pearl Street in 1811, and there he lived until he went back to Europe to fight with the allies against his old comrade in arms and to meet a soldier's death at the battle of Dresden. Hanover Square in Moreau's time boasted many stately residences. The Beekman house was not yet gone from No. 140 Pearl Street, and at No. 180, opposite Cedar, still stood the mansion of the De Peysters, the first head-quarters of Washington in the city of New York. When Abraham De Peyster built the latter house in 1696, it occupied an entire block planted with stately trees and looked through heavy shrubbery out upon the waters of the East River. Warehouses built on made ground long since hid the water front from view, but not until a recent period did the old house, with its stuccoed walls, tiled roof, and dormer windows, fall before the demands of business and of trade.

Continuing our walk through Pearl Street we come to Maiden Lane, threading the valley where the Dutch maidens washed their linen, and to the site of the famous Fly Market, so called because the burghers of the olden time pronounced their V's like F's, and said Fly for V'ly when they meant Valley. The Fly Market was set afoot in 1706 for the purpose of securing regular supplies and for fixing charges for meat and fish, and it remained for upward of a century one of the most frequented spots on Manhattan Island. The butchers of the Fly Market were sturdy fellows from the first, and a chapter could be written on their part in the history of the city. Such a chapter would have much to say of John Pessenger, an invincible patriot, who during the Revolution rendered substantial service by supplying meat to Washington's army, and in whose arms the gallant Leitch breathed out his life after the battle of Harlem Heights. Washington, who knew true worth wherever he came upon it, held Pessenger in high regard, and when as President he took up his residence in New York, he sought out his old friend at the Fly Market and gave him his trade. Henry Astor, elder brother of John Jacob, was a Fly Market butcher, and there laid the foundation of a comfortable fortune.

Grant Thorburn, New York's pioneer florist, also started business in this market. Thorburn was a Scotchman who, following his arrival in America in 1794, gave up the trade of nail-maker to become the keeper of a grocery store at the corner of Nassau and Liberty Streets. On an

April day in 1805 he saw a man for the first time selling flower-plants in the market. "As I carelessly passed along," he tells us in his autobiography, "I took a leaf, and, rubbing it between my fingers and thumb, asked him the name of it. He answered that it was a rose geranium. The plant had a pleasant smell, and I thought it would look well if removed into one of my green flower-pots, to stand on my counter to draw attention. Some one fancied and purchased plant and pot. The next day I went when the market was nearly over, judging that the man would sell cheaper, rather than have the trouble of carrying his stock over the river, as he lived at Brooklyn. Accordingly I purchased two plants, and having sold them, I began to think that something might be done in this way; and so I continued to go at the close of the market, and always bargained for the unsold plants. The man, finding me a useful customer, would assist me to carry them home, and show me how to shift the plants out of his pots and put them into green pots, if my customers wished it. Thus we wrought to one another's hands; and, from having one plant, in a short time I had fifty. People carrying their country friends to see the curiosities of the city would step in to see my plants. In some of these visits the strangers would express a wish to have some of these plants; but, having so far to go, could not carry them. Then they would ask for the seeds, but no one sold seed in New York, there being no market for an overplus. In this dilemma, I told my situation to the man from whom I had always bought the plants in the Fly Market. He said he was now raising seeds, with the intention of selling them next spring, along with his plants in the market; but if I would take his seeds, he would quit the market, and stay at home and raise plants and seeds for me to sell. A bargain was struck; I purchased his stock of seeds, amounting to fifteen dollars; and thus began a business that became the most extensive of the sort in the United States." The business founded by Thorburn existed until a few years ago at No. 15 John Street, on the site of the theatre built for the elder Hallam and his fellow-players.

Pushing northward from Maiden Lane, over paves darkened by the elevated railway, a walk of a few short blocks brings one to Franklin Square, and to the site, at No. 326 Pearl Street, of the Walton house, which stood until 1881 an imposing if shabby relic of the colonial period. This house was built about 1754 by William

Walton, a wealthy merchant of the town, and a "Member of His Majesty's Council for the Province of New York," who at his death left it to his nephew and namesake. We are told that when the elder Walton selected the site for it people wondered why he designed to build so far out of town, for at that time there was only one building on the south side of Pearl Street between Peck Slip and Cherry, and only four or five in the neighborhood of Franklin Square. He spared no expense in the erection and furnishing of his yellow brick and brownstone mansion, and, the fame thereof extending to England, it was cited in Parliament "as an example of colonial extravagance and a proof of the ability of the people to pay the royal taxes."

Set in ample gardens, which then ran down to the East River, with no intervening streets, the Walton house was fifty feet wide, with three stories and an attic, above which was a tiled and slightly sloping roof, encircled by two rows of balustrades. The main entrance, which boasted a massive portico with fluted columns surmounted by the arms of the Walton family, was in the middle of the building, and there were spacious drawing-rooms on each side of the wide mahogany staircase. Some of the rooms were panelled in oak, and the walls of others were hung with stamped and heavily gilded leather, while porcelain tiles set with flowers and birds adorned all of the fireplaces. The Walton house in the time of its first owner, whose portrait shows him as a man of robust build, attired in brown velvet coat, with long-flapped waistcoat of white satin, was the centre of a princely hospitality, and it continued for many years one of the show places of the town. Then an evil fate overtook it, and its last days were those of an overcrowded and dilapidated tenement.

The Walton house from 1784 to 1787 was occupied by the Bank of New York, the city's first bank, in whose organization Alexander Hamilton played a leading part. An early president of this institution was Isaac Roosevelt, whose house at No. 333 Pearl Street, just across the way, became after his death the city home of De Witt Clinton. This exceptional man dwelt there when mayor and recorder of the city, and there planned the work—the building of the Erie Canal—which gives him first place among the makers of modern New York. Twelve years mayor, four times governor, federal Senator, and candidate for President, Clinton was one of the master-spirits of his age. His work for city and

State was not unlike that which Hamilton accomplished for the nation, for not only a canal, but colleges, schools, asylums, and public societies found him a wise and helpful parent. He was deeply mourned when he died, but the people for whom he labored with such breadth of vision and such fruitful purpose have thus far neglected to rear a fitting monument to his memory.

The Walton and Roosevelt mansions are gone from Franklin Square, but the printing-house of the Harpers still abides there to link the present with the past. James Harper came to New York from a Long Island farm in 1810 to learn the printer's trade. He served his apprenticeship within a stone's throw of Franklin Square, and then set up for himself in a little room in Dover Street, where he was joined by his brother John. Their first task was the printing of two thousand copies of Seneca's "Morals" for Evert Duyckinck, the leading publisher of that day. Then they undertook a stereotyped edition of the Prayer-Book for the Episcopal Society of New York. They found, however, that they could not get the stereotyping done by others at a price that would assure them a profit; so they resolved to learn the art and do the work themselves. Their resolution cost them months of labor and many failures, but their task accomplished, it was pronounced the best piece of stereotyping ever seen in New York. It made the Harpers leaders in their business, and at the end of six years they were owners of the largest printing plant in the town. A third brother, Joseph Wesley, entered the firm in 1823; a fourth, Fletcher, was added in 1826; and these names constituted the house of Harper & Brothers for nearly fifty years.

The Harpers from printing for others, early passed to publishing ventures of their own, and with such success that when their original establishment was destroyed by fire in 1853, with a loss of three-quarters of a million dollars, they were able to replace it with the present building, and to continue to lead the publishing concerns of the country. Their imprint on a book fixed the reputation and often assured the fortune of its author. Time was when few American books were published that were not offered first to the Harpers; and it is only within recent years that they have been equalled or distanced by later comers in the publishing world. Moreover, such was the liberal spirit of its founders that those who entered their employ seldom left it,—men growing old in service only to be replaced by their sons; and among literary folk of a generation ago it was a common saying that if the Brothers Cheeryble had a house in New York it was located in Franklin Square.

Pearl Street ended in the old days at Chatham, and thence it is but a short walk to the pier of the Brooklyn bridge covering the site of the Cherry Street mansion which was the residence of Washington after his inauguration as President. The grimy Cherry Street of the present day, its tenements overflowing with a squalid army of the vicious poor, preserves in its name the memory of the time when it was a grass-grown lane threading a cherry orchard. Then it ran parallel with the river, to and into the Rutgers farm, which covered all the ground lying between Catherine and Montgomery Streets, and Division Street and the East River. A hundred and odd years ago Cherry Street was one of the most beautiful thoroughfares in the town, and a favorite place of residence. When New York was the federal capital, John Hancock lived at No. 5 Cherry Street, and twelve doors removed, on the same side of the way, lodged the officers of Washington's staff. William M. Tweed was born at No. 24, and No. 27 was long the residence of Captain Samuel Chester Reid, hero of the glorious fight at Fayal and

THE FIRST PRESIDENTIAL MANSION, NO. I CHERRY STREET, OCCUPIED BY WASHINGTON DURING THE FIRST SESSION OF THE FIRST CONGRESS

designer of the present plan of the American flag. Reid rests now in an unmarked grave in Greenwood, and his erstwhile home is a typical Cherry Street gin-mill.

Another short detour from Franklin Square, but this time into Frankfort Street, carries one to the heart of the region known since the early days as the Swamp. Wilhelmus Beekman came from Holland to New Amsterdam in 1647, and in a few years made himself owner of all the land now bounded by Nassau, Ann, Gold, Pearl, Fulton, and Frankfort Streets, and of the swamp below Pearl Street, which thereafter bore his name. In 1744 that part of Beekman's Swamp lying between Frankfort and Ferry and Cliff and Gold Streets became the property of Jacobus Roosevelt, who divided it into lots and sold them to tanners. The leather men prospered in the Swamp, and their successors are there to-day,—but with the modest tan-pits of pioneer times replaced by the largest leather warehouses in the world. The Hortons, Hoyts, and Pratts, the Lees, Knapps, and Lorillards were among the men who there won repute and fortune, and the Swamp has also furnished mayors, governors, and political leaders for city and State.

And it is a centre of story as well as of wealth

and commerce. Francis Lewis, a Welshman, who lived and carried on business as a tanner and furrier at the corner of Frankfort and William Streets, found himself at Oswego when it was attacked and captured by Montcalm. All the prisoners there taken were murdered by the Indians save Lewis, who, tradition has it, addressed the red men in Welsh, which sounded to them so much like their own tongue that they believed him a lost brother, and so spared his life. He survived to become a member of the Continental Congress and a signer of the Declaration of Independence. Nor has the Swamp been without its fads and bubbles. Fourscore years ago there flourished at No. 8 Jacob Street a locally famous spa. A running spring there discovered was believed to have various salutary properties. A Moorish building was put up over it; it became known as Jacob's Well, and ailing folk went to it every morning to partake of its waters at six pence a drink. But when some one found that the mineral qualities of the spring were due to its course through an old tan-pit its popularity declined, and the site was converted into a store.

Horace Greeley once lived among the tanners of the Swamp; Philip Freneau was born in Frankfort Street, and at the Carleton House, lately gone from the northeast corner of that thoroughfare and William Street, Charles Dickens lodged during his first visit to America. Dickens at that time was not quite thirty years old, but had already achieved a reputation of a kind such as no one before and no one since has compassed. Americans not only shared in the general admiration of the novelist, but many felt towards him a sentiment akin to personal affection; and when it was learned that he contemplated a visit to this country, Washington Irving, soon to depart for Spain, headed the list of authors who wrote to urge his coming.

Thus assured of a hearty welcome, Dickens sailed with his wife from Liverpool on January 4, 1842, landing eighteen days later at Boston. His reception in that city was enough to turn the head of an older man. Mrs. Dickens, writing home a few days after their arrival, spoke of it as "something not to be described," and added, "It will be the same, they tell us, all through America." And it was. In New York, whence he journeyed from Boston, all classes and conditions joined hands to welcome Dickens. There were parties and receptions in his honor; there was a dinner, presided over by Irving and attended by Bryant, Halleck, and many another;

and there was the famous "Boz" ball at the Park Theatre on February 14, 1842. "Kate and I," said Dickens, in a letter to his friend and biographer, John Forster, "were twice marched around before the ball began, escorted by Colden in evening dress, and by Morris"—the partner of Willis, but always prouder of his epaulets and sword than of his poetry and pen—"in a uniform of heaven knows what regiment of militia, while we were surrounded by three thousand people in full dress packed from roof to floor, with the house magnificently decorated, and amid lights, glitter, glare, show, noise, and cheering." New York folk for months thereafter talked of little else than the Dickens ball.

Twenty-five years after his first visit the novelist came again to America. In 1867 he determined to give a series of readings from his works in the United States, in order, as we know now, to recuperate an exchequer that had been too heavily drawn upon. These readings, from first to last, were an unparalleled success. Wherever he went great audiences crowded to greet him; and not less cordial were the personal welcomes,—welcomes which reached a fitting climax in the well-remembered press dinner given to him at Delmonico's on the night of April 18, 1868. This dinner represented authorship and journalism from Maine to Texas, and over the great West to California. It was a noble gathering,—two hundred guests from all parts of the Union, and all men of authority and renown. Horace Greeley presided, and opened the speaking in an address of persuasive eloquence and humor. He began by telling how more than thirty years before he had established a weekly paper called the *New Yorker*. "In looking about," said he, "for matter to fill my literary department I ran against some sketches from a cheap English periodical which I at once transferred to my paper. These sketches were by an unknown author, who wrote under the appellation of 'Boz.' So I think I can claim to be the first one who introduced Mr. Dickens to this country." Then he went on in his quaint, original way to tell how he had tried in a Florentine inn to read "David Copperfield" in Italian, ending with a toast that made every glass ring: "Health and happiness, honor, and generous because just recompense to our friend and guest, Charles Dickens."

When the cheering had died away Dickens arose to reply. He spoke amid the closest attention and at times enraptured applause. There was a figure at the end of his speech—it were better for America and England to go back to the ice age and be given over to the Arctic fox and bear than fight—that brought every guest to his feet; and as he sat down in a burst of cheers the band played "God Save the Queen." Four days later Dickens sailed for home. "Come to England when the hedges are in bloom and report at Gadshill," he said to a friend at the steamer's side. In June, 1870, this friend voyaged to England, and found the hedges in bloom, but—no master at Gadshill. Dickens had died three days before, and the American who had planned to be his guest was only in time to see the flowers still fresh on the slab above his grave in Westminster Abbey.

III

Along Lower Broadway

BROADWAY in the days when it was the Heere Straat of New Amsterdam was also the only highway that traversed the island from end to end, and such it remained for more than a century. A visitor set down in the Dutch town of 1664 would have found it flanked in its lower reaches with orchards and gardens and comfortable homes, and for the better part of two hundred years it continued to be a favorite and fashionable residence street. The Heere Straat became Broadway when Dutch gave way to English rule, and soon it was paved with stones and planted with trees as far as Trinity Church, erected in 1698 at the head of Wall Street. Beyond St. Paul's Chapel, at the corner of the present Vesey Street, Broadway in the later colonial period was known as Great George Street, and was so called until long after the Revolution. Our present pilgrimage may, therefore, begin at the Bowling Green and end in the neighborhood of St. Paul's.

The Washington Building at No. 1 Broadway holds the site of a house which remained until twenty years ago, one of the most interesting relics of olden days. John Watts, a man of mark in his era, built a fine house at what is No. 3 Broadway, where he lived with his wife. Ann Watts, their daughter, married Archibald Kennedy, captain in the British navy and afterwards Earl of Cassilis, and in 1750 my subsequent lord built No. 1 Broadway. We are told that on "great gala days and nights the two houses were connected by a bridge,—a rialto from which smiling belles looked upon the river which washed the foot of the garden. There was a carved door-way to the Kennedy mansion, a two-story-and-attic brick building, and it had wide halls and spacious rooms. The state drawing-room, fifty feet long, opened upon a porch in which a quadrille could be danced; and the dining-room was also vast and rich. And that nothing should be wanting to the loftiness of association, in this fine old house the eldest son of Archibald Kennedy and Ann Watts was born, to become not only twelfth Earl of Cassilis, but first Marquis of Ailsa."

The Kennedy house was a nerve-centre of history during the Revolution. April of 1776 brought Israel Putnam to command New York until Washington should arrive, and the stout old wolf-killer occupied No. 1 Broadway as his headquarters. Then it was that its walls became the prison of Margaret Moncrieff, daughter of an English engineer of distinction. Detained as a spy by the patriots, here the handsome maiden met and loved young Aaron Burr, aide-de-camp on Putnam's staff; nor in after years did she ever quite forget her hero of the blue and buff. She tells also in her memoir of having climbed to the roof of the house to watch the tents of the royal army on the Staten Island shore, and to pray for quick deliverance from her captors. Captain Kennedy had, the while, fallen on troubled times. His efforts to serve two masters earned him the ill-will of both, while his father-in-law, Watts, remaining loyal to the king, escaped the hands of the Sons of Liberty only to die in exile. Both men suffered the sequestration of their estates, and their heirs, such were the fortunes of war, were afterwards compelled to buy them back at exorbitant rates.

In the Kennedy house, after the Declaration of Independence was proclaimed, Washington gave audience to Colonel Patterson, sent by Lord Howe to see if an understanding could not still be reached between the crown and the colonies. He describes the patriot chieftain as a gentleman of noble presence, "elegantly attired" in full military costume. Patterson had brought with him a letter addressed to "George Washington, Esquire, etc., etc., etc.;" but rendered prudent by something in the manner of his host, he hastened to explain that the three et cæteras meant everything. "Indeed," said Washington, "they might mean anything;" adding that in his official capacity he could receive only letters officially addressed. To this Patterson could make no answer, as there was none to make, but, as he made ready to depart, asked if Washington had any message to send to Lord and General Howe. "Nothing," was the urbane reply, "but my particular compliments to both of them." General Howe afterwards declared that the interview was more polite than interesting, but it taught him, nevertheless, to change the superscription of his letters. Thereafter he took care to address Washington by his proper title.

Sir Henry Clinton and Sir Guy Carleton succeeded Washington as occupants of the Kennedy house, but Washington returned to it after the British evacuation, and from it went to Fraunces's Tavern to take leave of his officers. It was occupied after the Revolution by Isaac Sears, whilom leader of the Sons of Liberty; but in 1785 Sears fled the country a bankrupt, and a little later ended his stormy career in China.

The Kennedy house, while New York remained the federal capital, was the residence of Don Diego de Gardoqui, the Spanish embassador; and then, after serving for a time as a boarding-school for young ladies, became the home of Nathaniel Prime, counted in his day one of the richest men of the town. Prime began life as a coachman, but before middle age made himself the head of a great banking-house. Yet his end was a tragic one. Seized with the hallucination that his destiny was the almshouse, he cut his throat with a razor, and died on the instant. Then the Kennedy house became the Washington Hotel, and, as already noted, was in 1882 demolished for the erection of the present Washington Building.

Four doors removed, at what is now No. 9 Broadway, there stood in the old days the best known hostelry in the town. Martin Cregier, a man who played many parts in his time, and played most of them well, in 1649 built upon this spot a tavern which bore his name, and long remained the most frequented place of resort in the

Dutch hamlet. Cregier abandoned New York after its surrender to the English, and with his family moved to the Mohawk country, where he died in 1713, when far above the age of ninety. His tavern passed the while into other hands, and in 1763 we find Mrs. Steel, who had kept the King's Arms in Broad Street, removing to this house, to which she gave the name of her old place. Here is her announcement as it appeared in the *Post Boy:* "Mrs. Steel, Takes this method to acquaint her Friends and Customers, That the King's Arms Tavern, which she formerly kept opposite the Exchange, she hath now removed into Broadway (the lower end opposite the Fort), a more commodious house, where she will not only have it in her power to accommodate gentlemen with conveniences requisite as a tavern, but also, with genteel lodging apartments, which she doubts not will give satisfaction to every one who will be pleased to give her that honor." The King's Arms had many proprietors after Dame Steel rested from her labors, and, escaping the fires of 1776 and 1845, furnished until two-and-forty years ago a place for popular amusement. It bore in its last days the title of the Atlantic Garden.

Going a little farther afield, past the Columbia

Building, which at the northwest corner of Morris Street covers the graves of the Dutch pioneers, we come to Rector Street, so named because the residence of the rector of Trinity Church was established upon it, and whose Broadway corner in 1710 furnished a site for the second Lutheran Church reared in the city. This structure, destroyed in the fire of 1776, was succeeded in 1808 by the first building of Grace Church. A plain, square brick edifice, without turret, steeple, or cross, the original Grace Church, despite its modest outward seeming, was long the house of worship most affected by the wealth and fashion of the city. "Both young men and women," Dayton tells us, "fancied there was an air of quiet gentility in and about it not to be met with elsewhere, and 'I have attended Grace Church this morning' could not be uttered with a more satisfied air by a modern belle than the same sentence was spoken hundreds of times from beneath bonnets one of which would make headgear for the whole congregation of new Grace, if the gew-gaws with which they are ornamented could by any means be dispensed with."

The congregation of Grace Church removed in 1844 to Tenth Street and Broadway, and the

Rector Street corner was given over to business purposes. Old Trinity, however, still holds its ancient site a few yards away. It was in 1697, the eighth year of the reign of William and Mary, that a royal grant was made of a parcel of land "in or near to a street without the north gate of the city, commonly called the Broadway," for use "as the parish church and church-yard of the parish of Trinity Church, within our said city of New York." The church built on this grant was occupied in March, 1698, and its first resident rector was William Vesey, who for half a century continued as incumbent. The second rector was Henry Barclay. Samuel Auchmuty, the third rector, died in 1777 in the opening days of the Revolution. Charles Inglis, who succeeded Auchmuty, for his defiant loyalty to the crown was soon banished to England, and replaced by Samuel Provoost, an American educated in England. Benjamin Moore, who followed Provoost, was succeeded at his death by John Henry Hobart, and William Berrian, Hobart's successor, in 1862 by Morgan Dix, the present incumbent. Thus in two hundred years the church has had only nine rectors, each holding the office, on an average, for more than twenty years. Destroyed in the fire of 1776, the church was rebuilt two years later on the original site, with pews reserved for the President, the governor of the State, and members of Congress; but the second building was found to be unsafe in 1839, and seven years later was replaced by the present structure.

The grant in 1705 of the Queen's Farm made Trinity the wealthiest parish in America, and also enabled it to become the generous mother of many children. St. Paul's in Broadway, St. John's in Varick Street, St. Agnes's in Ninety-second Street, St. Augustine's in Houston Street, St. Chrysostom's in West Thirty-ninth Street, St. Luke's in Hudson Street, and Trinity Chapel in West Twenty-fifth Street are all included in Trinity parish and wholly maintained by it. Besides these churches, the parish contributes to the support of many others, and to various missions. It also maintains Trinity Infirmary in Varick Street, and five beds in St. Luke's Hospital for the sick poor, for whom a burial-place is provided at Newtown, Long Island, and there are five scholarships at Trinity College, Hartford, to which the rector nominates, the holders being relieved from all expenses during the course, except such as are personal. The income received from what remains to the parish of the land included in Queen Anne's grant, exceeds half a million dollars a year, and this splendid revenue is administered in no niggardly spirit. A large part of it is expended on the estate, upward of a tenth is given to poor churches outside the parish, and not one dollar is hoarded.

Thus Old Trinity, with its history in a measure the history of the city, possesses an affectionate interest for every lover of all that is uplifting in the past; and this interest is quickened and deepened by memory of the heroic dead who take their rest in its burial-garth. The ground to the north of the church contains many thousands of unmarked graves, for here during the British occupation of New York, between 1776 and 1783, uncounted numbers of patriot soldiers who perished in the prison-pens of the city were buried in trenches. Tradition has it that the graves of most of these men are thirty feet below the surface of the graveyard; and that by successive fillings, as the ground became full of human remains, it reached its present height.

Thus the thickly clustering tombstones tell only half the story of the great army buried in this place. About, above, and mingling with the unknown dead, however, are many whose names still remain on the tablets of stone. Here lies all that is mortal of Robert Livingston, whom Jacob Milborne impleaded for his murder at heaven's bar; of Michael Cresap, a renowned Indian fighter of colonial times; of Alexander Hamilton, Albert Gallatin, and William, Earl of Stirling; of John Morin Scott, John Lamb, and Marinus Willett, founders and leaders of the Sons of Liberty; of Philip Livingston and Francis Lewis, signers of the Declaration of Independence; of Robert Fulton and General Phil Kearny, who ended his gallant career at Chantilly; and of Charlotte Temple, the unhappy heroine of Mrs. Rowson's pathetic tale. Here also rests Captain James Lawrence, whose last words, "Don't give up the ship," gave him a place in America's Valhalla; and his widow sleeps beside him, the inscription above her grave recording only her name and the date of her birth and burial. She was but twenty-five when her husband mounted into history from the deck of the "Chesapeake," and she lived for half a century in her widowhood.

In the days when Old Trinity was still young the De Lancey house, one of the largest and finest structures in the town, faced Broadway from the northern corner of the present Thames Street. On the southern side of the same street stood the mansion of the Van Cortlands, with their stone sugar-house in the rear. The Trinity and the Boreel Buildings now cover these sites, —the Boreel standing on that of the old De Lancey house. The builder of this house, a two-storied structure of graystone sloping down to the shore of the Hudson, was Etienne De Lancey, founder in America of the family of the name, and from him it passed to his son, James De Lancey, long lieutenant-governor and virtual ruler of the province. The younger De Lancey made it for many years the centre of a stately hospitality, but in 1754 leased it to Edward Willett, a well-known publican of the period, who converted it into a hostelry under the name of the Province Arms. The new tavern leaped at once into popular favor. In 1763 one John Crawley was its landlord; but in 1765, the year of the Stamp Act excitement, he was succeeded by George Burns from the King's Head at the Whitehall; and it was in Burns's Long Room at the Province Arms that on October 31 upward of two hundred merchants of the town signed an agreement to import no more goods from England until the obnoxious act should be repealed. Burns's place was taken in 1770 by Richard Bolton, who migrated from the Queen's

Head in Pearl Street, and whose brief tenancy was made memorable by a number of imposing balls and receptions,—notably one given to John Murray, Earl of Dunmore, upon the occasion of his arrival to take command of the province.

In 1771 Bolton was followed in the management of the Province Arms by Robert Hull, who renamed it the City Arms. "Through all the tramp and bustle of the Revolution," Stevens tells us, "it continued to hold its own as the chief tavern of the town. The officers of the British army, brilliant in their scarlet uniforms, thronged the porch and piazzas, while the girls, who loved the military, paced the Church Walk, as the walk in front of Trinity was called, in evening promenade. Within, the usual revelry and festivity of a garrison town. On one occasion the old walls were the witness of a terrible tragedy. It was an evening in late September. During the day a fleet of men-of-war, with a heavy convoy of provisions and supplies, had entered the harbor. A difference had occurred during the voyage between Captain Tollemache (brother of the Earl of Dysart), the commander of the 'Zebra' man-of-war, and Captain Pennington, of the Coldstream Guards. The offence was a sonnet written by Captain Pennington, which Captain

Tollemache took up as reflecting upon the wit of his lady. Suspended at sea by the necessities of the service, the quarrel was renewed on shore. The meeting took place at the tavern. A brace of pistols were first fired without result, when swords were drawn. Tollemache was run through the breast, and instantly expired, while Pennington, who received seven wounds, survived the encounter." The body of Tollemache was buried in Trinity church-yard.

With the departure of the English, John Cape leased the old tavern, and hung out the State Arms of New York; and on December 2, 1783, its walls witnessed the first great entertainment given to Washington after the declaration of peace. Thereafter, under divers hosts, it maintained its reputation until 1792, when it passed into the hands of the Tontine Association, and was demolished to furnish a site for the famous house known as the City Hotel. What the Astor House was to the middle the City Hotel was to the opening years of the New York of the last century. A plain four-storied structure, occupying the entire front of the block bounded by Thames and Cedar Streets, it remained for the better part of threescore years not only the best-known house of entertainment in the city, but travellers asserted it had no equal in the land. Substantial comfort, Dayton tells us, was the ruling motive of its management, "and in no instance was that paramount essential lost sight of to make room for senseless display. The wine-room of the old hotel was a well-known institution, and its memory is still cherished by those who in youth tasted its rare stores. Its shelves were loaded tier upon tier with the choicest vintages the nicest taste could call, and the selections were pronounced by connoisseurs as unsurpassed in purity or flavor. Jennings and Willard were the proprietors of this far-famed hotel. Willard's station was in the office, where from sunrise to midnight he was ever faithful at his post; and such was his activity of mind and body that his complex dutics of host, clerk, book-keeper, cashier, bar-keeper, and heaven only knows what besides, were bustled through, not only with apparent ease but with the most unruffled good nature. The best-known man in the city, nevertheless his world lay within the walls of his hostelry, and he would have been compelled to inquire his way if he had been placed by himself a stone's throw from the City Hotel. Jennings was the unseen but by no means the unimportant partner in the management of the hotel. His quiet duties were to provide supplies and to superintend the details from cellar to garret. In the dining-room he was commander-in-chief, and the silent clock-work of his subordinates might be imitated to advantage in many modern establishments where pompous head-waiters strut about in imitation of the guests who were present to meet Mr. Samuel Weller, when he partook of the soiree prepared in his honor by the select footmen of Bath." The history of the City Hotel came to an end in 1850, when it was torn down and replaced by a block of stores.

The quaint houses and quainter shops which kept it company in the old days have likewise been swept away, and St. Paul's Church between Vesey and Fulton Streets is the one visible link binding the Broadway of the present to the Broadway of the century before the last. Built in 1764, St. Paul's has witnessed every change that has since swept over the city, and in its burial-plot sleep scores of men and women who played an honorable part in the making of the town. These are not unremembered, but no monumental inscription is so often read as the one against the chancel end of the church and facing Broadway, which records the services of

General Richard Montogmery, the gallant Irishman, who when he fell at Quebec, at the early age of thirty-eight, stood second only to Washington in the esteem of the patriot leaders. One's eyes fill with tears when reading the story of Montgomery and his bride. A captain in the British army, he had met Janet Livingston, sister of the chancellor, while on his way to serve under Wolfe at Louisburg; and when, a few years later, he returned to settle in America, he renewed his acquaintance with and married her. There still exists the quaintly worded letter in which the soldierly seeker for a fair maiden's hand sought her father's consent to the union. "Finding," he writes, "that you have already had intimation of my desire to be honored with your daughter's hand, and apprehensive lest my silence should bear an unfavorable construction, I have ventured at last to request, sir, that you will consent to a union which to me has the most promising appearance of happiness, from the lady's uncommon merit and amiable worth. Nor will it be an inconsiderable addition to be favored by such respectable characters with the title of son, should I be so fortunate as to deserve it. And if to contribute to the happiness of a beloved daughter can claim any share with tender parents, I hope hereafter to have some title to your esteem."

"We approve of your proposal, and heartily wish that your union may yield you the happiness you seem to expect," was the father's answer. And so they were married in July, 1773. Following his marriage, Montgomery settled at Rhinebeck, where he built a mill and laid the foundation of a house. Then the Revolution broke in upon his quiet and domestic happiness. He was among the first brigadier-generals created by Congress, and was a little later detailed as one of the leaders of the expedition against Quebec. He was reluctant to leave his home, but his heart was in the movement for independence. "My honor is engaged," he told his wife, "and you shall never blush for your Montgomery." And so they parted, he to die at the gates of Quebec and she to survive in lonely widowhood for more than fifty years. Montgomery was buried within the walls of Quebec with the honors of war, but in 1818 his remains, at public request, were disinterred and brought down the Hudson for reburial in St. Paul's. Word was sent to the widow that the funeral-boat would arrive opposite her house at a certain time, so that she could be ready to look down from the portico and see what was forever beyond her wish. "At length," she wrote in a letter to her niece, "they came by with all that remained of a beloved husband, who left me in the bloom of manhood, a perfect being. Alas! how did he return! However gratifying to my heart, yet to my feelings every pang I felt was renewed. The pomp with which it was conducted added to my woe. When the steamboat passed with slow and solemn movement, stopping before my house, the troops under arms, the Dead March from the muffled drums, the mournful music, the splendid coffin canopied with crape and crowned by plumes, you may conceive my anguish; I cannot describe it." The flood of memories rushing upon the aged woman's brain caused her to fall upon the ground, and there, when the cortege had passed, they found her lying as insensible as her husband's dust.

The building of the Astor House, just across the way from St. Paul's, assured to its owner a larger meed of fame than did any other achievement of his fruitful career. The pioneer of the palaces which have made the American hotel known and admired throughout the world, its opening in 1836 was called at the time "a prodigious and costly event," and was attended by all the magnates of the city. Not without reason, for it at once became and long remained the stopping-place of all the distinguished people who came to New York. Andrew Jackson, Sam Houston, Daniel Webster, Henry Clay, and Abraham Lincoln, along with Irving, Hawthorne, and Dickens, Macready, Rachel, and Jenny Lind, were guests of its early days; and there are few familiar names in the history of the country between 1836 and 1902 whose owners have not found lodging within its portals. Time was when the Astor House was the rendezvous not only of politicians and public officials, but of all the literary men in the town. Walt Whitman delighted to bask on its steps and watch the omnibuses, when, as Tuckerman phrases it, you could walk from Barnum's to the Battery on their roofs, while Poe, when editor of *Graham's Magazine,* often went there for refreshment and for news, and there during the Mary Rogers excitement caught the idea which he embodied in the tale of "Marie Roget."

Memories not less notable are called to mind by the name of the man who for the better part of forty years directed the fortunes of this famous hostelry. The affairs of the Astor House did not run smoothly at the outset, and its owner looked about for some one who could mend them. A young New Englander, Charles Stetson by name, had proved his ability as a hotel-keeper, and Astor sent for him. Stetson obeyed the summons, to be measured from head to foot by the old merchant, who finally said,—

"I understand you want to do some business with me, young man."

"No," was the answer; "I understood you wanted to transact some business with me. Your clerk wrote me a note asking me to call; but if you have no business with me, I will bid you good morning."

"Sit down, young man; don't be in such a hurry. What are you going to do, young man?"

"I am going to get my living, and get it by hotel-keeping."

"And you think you can keep my hotel?"

"Yes, I can keep any hotel. I will keep a hotel,—not a tavern."

"And what is the difference between a tavern and a hotel, young man?"

"Just the difference between what your hotel is and what you wish it to be. A tavern-keeper knows when to go to market and how to feed so many people. A hotel-keeper is a gentleman who stands on a level with his guests."

"I think we can do business, young man. Let's come to terms."

Stetson said he was without means to buy out the lessees and put the hotel in running order.

"And how much money will you want?" asked the old man.

"I may not want more than one thousand dollars, I may want twenty; but I will not take the house unless I can draw on you for fifty thousand dollars if I need it. I will buy the lease if it costs me twenty thousand dollars, and put the house in order if it costs me another twenty thousand."

"Fifty thousand dollars is a good deal of money," said Astor; "and I have no security."

"You have my honor and the promise that I will keep what you want,—a first-class hotel."

Stetson's terms were acceded to, and thus he became the proprietor of the Astor House, and the host and friend as well of half of the eminent men of his time.

Another name inseparably associated with the early history of the Astor House is that of Thurlow Weed, who long made it his New York home. Weed holds a place apart in political history. Save for brief service as a legislator in early manhood, he held no public place, yet he was more a maker of office-holders than any man of his time, and for upward of thirty years his smile and frown were the delight and terror of all place-seekers along the Hudson. He was the editor during the same period of the *Albany Evening Journal,* but he was always rather a politician than a journalist, and he relied more upon the private arts of the one than the public appeals of the other. Between 1830 and 1860 there was no State or national convention of his party—first the Whig and later the Republican—where his influence was not displayed, no nomination about which he was not consulted, and no successful election in whose arrangements he did not bear a part. He had admirable tact and quick insight into character, he knew how to mould and control men, and he led by seeming to follow. An anecdote cited by Browne illustrates his adroit dealing with stubborn spirits. A contumacious member of the legislature hated Weed and often declared that he took no one's opinions but his own. Weed, wanting the man's vote, introduced himself one morning in this wise:

"I have often heard of you. I know you don't like me, and I respect your candor. I always esteem an open enemy. You are one of the few men who are self-reliant, have wills of their own, and won't be influenced by others. I like that, too; I recognize in you a kindred spirit. We won't and can't agree, but that is no reason why we should quarrel. Drop in and see me. I enjoy original men. You see I know you. If you won't be influenced by me, perhaps I can learn something from you."

The resolute assemblyman at the end of a month was under the complete dominion of Weed, but believing also that the latter had taken his counsel. Weed had a hand in the making of half a dozen Presidents, and in his room at the Astor House—No. 11 on the parlor floor—cabinets were built, foreign embassies arranged, candidates created or destroyed, and distribution made of the patronage of State and nation. Late in life Weed became a permanent resident of New York, and his tall figure, with the massive head and benevolent features, was long a familiar object in public places. His home was No. 12 West Twelfth Street, and there he died in 1882 at the age of eighty-five.

One other historic landmark awaits the pilgrim along and about lower Broadway,—St. Peter's Church in Barclay Street, which holds the site of the first Catholic place of worship reared in New York. That faith, as we know, was under ban during the greater part of the colonial period, and it was not until after the Revolution that Catholics enjoyed free exercise of their religion. Before that time arrest and imprisonment were the lot of any priest who openly celebrated the Mass. When complete toleration came with independence, one Father Farmer gathered a little flock about him, and for a time held services in a carpenter-shop on Barclay Street. Then, emboldened by growth in numbers, the congregation purchased lots on the corner of Barclay and Church Streets, and in October, 1785, the corner-stone of a church was laid with appropriate ceremonies. Tradition has it that Charles III. of Spain contributed a large sum towards the erection of the structure.

St. Peter's was consecrated in 1786, and until the building of St. Patrick's in 1809, at the corner of Mott and Mulberry Streets, it remained the only Catholic Church on Manhattan Island. It gave way in 1836 to the present building, which looks far older than its years, but the vanished church will ever hold a place in the reverent regard of the followers of a faith whose wonderful growth, both in numbers and influence, has been a distinguishing feature of the life of the city during the last fourscore years.

IV

Wall Street in Early Days

THERE was great excitement, with much running to and fro, in New Amsterdam on March 13, 1653, for out of the East had come the rumor that the New Englanders, a race regarded by all honest Dutchmen with a hate that had in it something of fear, were planning a foray on the town. This was a peril that called for heroic measures, and Stuyvesant, who loved a fight best of all things, rose to the occasion in a manner befitting the dignity of his office. He appointed a day of general fasting and prayer, and he called a meeting of his council, with the burgomasters and schepens attending, which at the end of a long morning's session resolved "that the whole body of citizens shall keep watch by night, in such places as shall be designated, the City Tavern to be the temporary head-quarters; that the Fort shall be repaired; that Captain Vischer shall be requested to fix his sails, to have his piece loaded, and to keep his vessel in readiness; and that because the Fort is not large enough to contain all of the inhabitants, it is deemed necessary to enclose the greater part of the city with upright palisades and a small breast-work, so that in case of necessity all the inhabitants may retire therein, and, as far as practicable, defend themselves and their property from attack."

Then, having also prepared a list for a forced levy, by which the sum of five thousand guilders was to be raised for purposes of defence, councilmen, burgomasters, and schepens rested from their labors until the third day, when specifications for the proposed palisades were prepared and adopted. Work thereon was at once begun, and May-day of 1653 saw its successful conclusion. The wall thus brought into being was about one hundred and eighty rods long, and, after running for a short distance along the East River, it extended, as we know, straight across the island to the North River, following the line of a fence built by Director Kieft to keep the cattle of the townsfolk from wandering out of their joint pasture-lands. Three years later two gates were built in the wall,—the Water Gate at the junction of the present Pearl and Wall Streets, and the Land Gate at the corner of Broadway and Wall Street. The New Englanders, however, came not to attack the town, and hostile hand was never laid upon the defence planned for their undoing. The English, when they became masters of the city, repaired and extended Stuyvesant's wall; but in 1685 a street was surveyed and ordered to be established along its line, and in 1699 we find the citizens petitioning for its final demolition, saying, "Whereas the former line of fortifications that ranged along Wall Street from the East River to the North River are fallen to decay, and the encroachments of buildings which have been made adjacent thereto will render the same useless for the future, and the city proposing with all speed to build a new City Hall at the end of one of the streets, fronting the above said line of fortifications, we pray His Excellency that the said fortifications be demolished, and the stones of the bastions be appropriated to building the said City Hall."

The prayer was granted, and the corner-stone of the new City Hall laid with much ceremony in the same autumn. Another year brought its practical completion at a cost of four thousand pounds. It was a notable building for that time, being supported upon brick arches, under which pedestrians could pass from street to street. One of the rooms on the first floor, cut in twain by a large corridor, was used at a later period to house the city's first fire-engines, and there was a dungeon in the rear for all prisoners save debtors. The court-room, the jury-room, and the room for the common council occupied the second floor. The attic for three-fourths of a century was used as a debtors' prison, while, to make the terrors of the law more impressive to offenders, in 1703 the cage, pillory, stocks, and whipping-post, which had flanked the Stadt Huys at the water's edge, were removed to the upper end of Broad Street and placed close to the City Hall. Yet another speaking proof of the harsh conditions of colonial times was the slave-mart that in 1709 was established at the foot of Wall Street. "All negroes and Indian slaves that are let out to hire within the city," ran an ordinance adopted in 1731, "shall take up their standing in the market-house at the Wall Street Slip, until such time as they are hired, whereby all persons may know where to hire slaves as their occasion shall require." Slaves were also bought and sold there, and it was not until 1762 that the residents of the street found courage to complain of the mart and to demand its removal.

The City Hall made Wall Street for nearly a century the centre of municipal and provincial affairs. Above and below it as time went on one goodly dwelling after another was built and occupied, and the wealth and position of their owners helped to invest the thoroughfare with peculiar attractions. There abode the McEvers, whose mansion stood at the northeast corner of William Street, and there also were the imposing homes of the Marstons, Van Hornes, Buchanans, Dennings, and Cuylers. Finally, in 1764, whipping-posts, stocks, cage, and pillory were transferred to the Common, and all doubts removed from Wall Street's claim to be the fashionable residence thoroughfare of the town.

During the troubled days that followed the passage of the Stamp Act and the opening of the Revolution more than one stirring incident had Wall Street for its background. The Stamp-Act Congress assembled in the City Hall, in the room where thirty years before Andrew Hamilton had pleaded the cause of John Peter Zenger and sounded the defiance of royal authority which had its echo in Yorktown. It was also in the City Hall that on a December day in 1773 the chief men of the town met to decide whether or not they should pay the duty a stubborn king had caused to be imposed upon tea. John Lamb, we are told, read the act of Parliament to the assembled throng, and called for an expression of opinion as to whether obedience should be rendered, when shouts of "No! No! No!" thrice repeated instantly shook the building from floor to rafter, and "left no doubt as to the sense of the meeting." Less than two years later, on a Sunday morning in April, came the news of Concord and Lexington, and with it the prompt confiscation by the Sons of Liberty of the arms and ammunition stored in one of the chambers of the City Hall. A second Sunday morning in the same spring, such were the passions of the time, saw the appearance in Wall Street of a hundred and fifty armed men, who with drums beating and fifes playing paraded up and down from Broadway to the East River, and back again, after which they marched into Trinity Church, resolved upon making the rector, Rev. Charles Inglis, forego his prayers for the king and the royal family. The clergyman manfully refused to omit any part of the service, and no harm was done him, but the members of the vestry pacified their visitors with the promise that the church should be closed until a more peaceful time. This was the last public service held within its walls, which were reduced to ruins in the great fire of the following year.

Wall Street witnessed yet another memorable incident before the occupation of the city by the British,—the reading on July 18, 1776, from the steps of the City Hall, and by order of the Provincial Congress, of the Declaration of Independence. Eight days before, by direction of Washington, this document had been read at the head of each brigade of the Continental army; but the ceremony at the City Hall voiced in an especial way the sentiments of the people of New York and borrowed significance from the fact that the fleet of the enemy then lay at anchor in the harbor, and that the women and children, along with the aged and infirm, were being hurried from the city in anticipation of an early conflict. Thousands, nevertheless, gathered to listen to the reading, and filled the air with their huzzas; nor did the more hot-headed ones rest content until they had torn the royal coat of arms from the wall of the City Hall, and burned it in a bonfire kindled for the purpose.

Wall Street suffered heavily during the years the city lay in the thrall of the enemy. Men from the ranks of the invading army broke open and looted the City Hall, while the stately houses which kept it company, vacated by their patriot owners, furnished quarters for the British and

Hessian officers, and suffered rough and untidy usage. There was quick recovery, however, after the evacuation, and Wall Street had regained much of its whilom comeliness when in December, 1784, New York became the capital of the confederacy. Congress held its sessions in the City Hall, and there John Jay, lately come from Europe, organized our foreign affairs on a modest scale, but with a grasp of essentials that won for the infant nation the respect of crowns and kingdoms. Then came the framing and adoption of the Constitution, and the election and inauguration of Washington as first President of the republic.

The City Hall, enlarged and adorned for its new honors, now became Federal Hall, and furnished a meeting-place for House and Senate. Thither Washington drove in coach-and-six to deliver in person his messages to Congress, and to afterwards record in his diary that "in the rear came the chief justice, and the secretaries of the treasury and war departments in their respective carriages, and in the order they are named." Alexander Hamilton, after Washington the most potential figure in the government, was one of a score of federal officials and foreign ministers who at that period resided in Wall Street. His modest house stood upon part of the present site of the Mechanics' Bank, and next to the northeast corner of William Street was the more imposing residence of General John Lamb, then and for years afterwards collector of the port.

Wall Street's political and social glory waned when the seat of government was transferred to Philadelphia on the way to the banks of the Potomac; but the same decade marked the opening of its history as a centre of finance. The Tontine Building at the corner of Water Street furnished after 1794 a meeting-place for the merchants and traders of the town, and in 1798 the Bank of New York, which had begun business at the old Walton house in Pearl Street, removed to the McEvers mansion, at the corner of William Street, the same site which it occupies at the present time. One by one other financial institutions had their birth in or made their way to Wall Street. The first Merchants' Exchange was built in 1827, and seven years later the general government bought the site of the old City Hall and reared thereon the structure first used as a custom-house, but the home since 1863 of the sub-treasury. The adjoining building, originally occupied by the United States Bank of stormy memory, became the assay-office in

TRINITY CHURCH AND FEDERAL HALL, WALL STREET, 1789—DRAWN BY DAVID GRIM

1854, and the same twelvemonth saw the setting afoot of the clearing-house, which time and growth have made the most powerful banking organization in America, if not in the world.

While the seal was thus being placed upon Wall Street's supremacy in finance, another of its famous institutions—the stock exchange—passed from struggling youth to lusty manhood. Treasured in the archives of the exchange is the original agreement of its founders, dated May 17, 1792, saying, "We the subscribers, brokers for the purchase and sale of public stock, do hereby solemnly promise and pledge ourselves to each other that we will not buy or sell from this day, from any person whatsoever, any kind of public stock at a less rate than one-quarter per cent. commission on the special value, and that we will give a preference to each other in our negotiations." This was signed by twenty-four brokers, who met under a buttonwood-tree in front of what is now the Central Trust Company Building, at No. 60 Wall Street. Most of the stock transactions were then made in the coffee-rooms and taverns of the neighborhood. The brokers, following this agreement, met for a time in each other's offices, but in 1817 hired an upper room in the Merchants' Exchange. Four years later they adopted a new and more elaborate constitution, after the model of a similar and older organization in Philadelphia, and for the first time imposed an entrance-fee of twenty-five dollars. To-day a seat in the board is worth thrice as many thousands.

The New York Stock and Exchange Board, as the brokers' association soon came to be called, was driven from its first recognized home by the great fire of 1835, and for several years held its sessions in a hall in Jauncey Court, but in 1842 returned to the new Merchants' Exchange, now the custom-house. It removed eleven years later to rooms in the old Corn Exchange Bank, at Beaver and William Streets, and from thence to quarters in Lord's Court, Exchange Place, where it was located during the panic of 1857 and at the outbreak of the Civil War.

The exchange for many years refused admission to new members, and held its daily meetings behind closed doors. This policy led about 1837 to the organization of the Open Board of Brokers, whose members, denied entrance to the regular body, sought by every expedient ingenuity could devise to learn its doings and quotations. The new organization died when the older one hid itself on the top floor of the Corn Exchange Bank, but in 1863 a second open board of brokers was established in a William Street basement known as the "Coal-Hole." This throve apace, and moving the while to roomy quarters in Broad Street, by 1869 had acquired fully one-half the speculative business done on "the street." Finally, in May, 1869, warfare between the old and the new ended in consolidation, and both were housed in the edifice that had been built for the parent body in December, 1865. This marble building occupies a portion of the space between Broad and New Streets, and has also an entrance on Wall Street.

There were many uncommon men among the early members of the stock exchange, but none more remarkable than Jacob Little, whose career had more of dash and originality in it than Wall Street has ever seen in any other man. The son of a bankrupt father, Little came to New York from his native Newburyport in 1817, and at the end of five years passed in the employ of others opened a broker's office in a small basement in Wall Street. There he labored as few men labor, and with a self-reliance and a foresightedness beyond his years. He joined the stock exchange in 1825, and another decade saw him the best known and the most fearless of its operators, his methods bringing him while he was still young a fortune mounting into the millions. Three times he became a bankrupt, but recovered after each failure, and paid every creditor in full, so that it became a common saying that "Jacob Little's suspended papers were better than the checks of most men."

A hundred stories of this doughty speculator still make the rounds of Wall Street. Erie upon one occasion was a favorite stock, and was selling at par. Little threw himself against the street, and contracted to sell a large amount of this stock for future delivery. His rivals, bent upon his undoing, took all the contracts he offered, bought up all the new stock, and, as they believed, made it impossible for him to redeem his contracts. Still Little continued to sell the stock short, thousands upon thousands of shares, and when friends pointed out the plot against him, bade them take no thought for his welfare. Then came the day, fixed by the rules, when the stock he had sold must be delivered. The street for a block beyond his office door was jammed at an early hour by men awaiting his arrival and their share in his assets. Little came upon the scene, calm and self-reliant, and, pushing his way through the throng, entered the building. An hour passed after he shut the door behind him, and every moment's delay was accepted as proof that he would now confess that he must go to the wall. Prices, in the face of this belief, continued to mount upward, and every second added a point to the quotations. There were some brokers, however, who seemed to yet have faith in Little, and as the price rose contracts were entered into after a fashion that astounded everybody who did not know Little himself was directing this further skirmish. Then, as the clock struck ten, the office door flew open and disclosed Little behind the counter, a stock of parchment at his right hand. This parchment was new Erie stock, and soon the crowd made discovery that something was wrong. Little kept nobody in doubt.

"The fact is," said he, "I haven't really been short of the stock, for I had a few millions of Erie bonds, and they were convertible into stock. That is the reason I did not get scared, you see."

A panic followed this announcement. Little, with an unlimited quantity of stock on hand, was not only able to offer to fulfill every contract, but he also bought back at a fall in price all the stock he had sold at par. Half the houses in Wall Street were heavy losers, and Little retained his leadership. His methods, however, finally hurled him down and beat him to pieces. He was an aging man when failure overtook him for the fourth time, and he went out of life as poor as he had entered it.

The career of Daniel Drew was not unlike that of Little, and it had a yet more tragic conclusion. Drew left his father's farm in Putnam County, New York, at the age of fifteen, and served as a private soldier during the second war with England. Then he became a buyer of cattle, and, prospering from the first, in 1829 established his head-quarters at Bull's Head in the Bowery, which he made the Drovers' Exchange. His operations were not limited to New York, and great droves of cattle crossed the Alleghanies under his direction. He engaged while still a young man in steamboat enterprises, and in 1840 established the People's Line on the Hudson. Before this he had appeared in Wall Street, where from the first his operations proved his cunning and his boldness. Winning millions with the years, he became a large stockholder in the Erie company, and its treasurer. Drew's associates on 'change often called him the "great bear," for he had an especial knack of selling Erie stock short and then as treasurer issuing to himself great blocks of stock, which he would dump on the market to the confusion of the bulls. Indeed, so great was his power that he often advanced or depressed Erie stock thirty per cent. in the course of a day. He at one time controlled more ready cash than any one man in America, and what he did not know about the market was supposed to be beyond the province of human knowledge. But towards the close of his career and on an evil day for himself Drew made the acquaintance of two young men, named Jay Gould and James Fisk. Something less than five years later he who had been a multi-millionaire died a broken-hearted bankrupt,—his entire assets a Bible and a hymn-book.

The same story could be told of other once famous operators,—of Henry N. Smith, of Lawrence Jerome, of Alden B. Stockwell, of Samuel Mills, of John Pondir, and of John A. Tobin,—and there is a tradition in the street that the man who speculates never ends a winner. Ex-Police Superintendent Walling, when writing his book of reminiscences, made a careful investigation of this theory, and found only one man, a Rhode Islander named Smith, who had quit speculation with more money than when he entered it. He had won thirty thousand dollars in a single deal, and had then returned satisfied to his home, his experience the one bright incident in a melancholy record of wreckage.

Wall Street history, nevertheless, has its inspiring as well as its gloomy passages. The express companies of America had their origin on a May day in 1840, when Alvin Adams journeyed from Boston to New York, carrying on his person a small sum of money he was to pay and a few notes which he was to collect. The business thus begun was conducted for a twelvemonth in the smallest possible way, a couple of carpet-bags sufficing for the stowage of the packages intrusted to its founder's care. Then William B. Dinsmore became the New York partner of Adams, with an office in the neighborhood of Wall Street, and with the rapid increase of business branches were established in Philadelphia, Baltimore, and other cities. Twelve years later Adams and Dinsmore's modest venture had expanded into a wealthy and powerful corporation with arms stretching out towards all the towns and villages in the land. Among the early employees of the company thus brought into being, was a lively lad who cried papers on the street when that was an uncertain calling, but who was ever ready to hold a horse or run an errand to earn a small gratuity. Happy chance brought this boy under the eye of Adams, and upon due trial he became a fixture in the business. His name was John Hoey, and, growing with his opportunities, he remained until ripe old age the directing spirit of the great business with which he had been associated from its inception and his earliest boyhood.

Wall Street was also the home of many of the early newspapers of the city. The *Journal of Commerce* for a quarter of a century occupied the southeast corner of Wall and Water Streets, and a building on the north side of Wall Street between Pearl and William was long the office of the *Courier and Inquirer.* David Hale and Gerard Hallock were the proprietors of the former and James Watson Webb of the latter journal. Webb had been a soldier in his youth, and though the *Courier and Inquirer* showed ability and enterprise under his conduct, whenever the productions of his own pen appeared in its columns they usually wore a decidedly belligerent garb. A duel, in which he himself stood as one of the principals, grew out of this habit of plain speech. Thomas F. Marshall, of Kentucky, declared on the floor of Congress that Webb had accused him and other members of bribery. Webb wrote a private letter to Marshall denying that he had made such a charge, and showing that Marshall had been misled by the comments of another newspaper. He advised Marshall to read the original article, learn the truth, and retract what he had said in his speech. No reply was made to this letter.

Marshall soon after came to New York to defend a noted forger, and Webb, who believed he had been unfairly treated, commented sharply in his newspaper on the conduct of a member of Congress in leaving his seat to appear at the bar of a distant criminal court. Day after day the *Courier and Inquirer* continued its attacks upon Marshall, who the night before he was to sum up for his client addressed a note to Webb inviting him to be present in court on the following day. The editor appeared, and Marshall denounced him in a stinging phillipic. Webb's comments on this speech proved too much for Marshall to bear, and there followed a challenge and a hostile meeting in Delaware. Webb's first shot was below and his second just above his opponent's feet. Marshall's first shot went wide of its mark, but the second one took effect in Webb's knee, inflicting a wound from which he never fully recovered. Webb, on returning to

New York, was indicted for leaving the State to fight a duel, found guilty, despite the efforts of able counsel, and sentenced to two years imprisonment. Much sympathy, however, was manifested for him, many of his bitterest political enemies signing petitions for his release, and, after he had spent a fortnight in the Tombs, Governor Seward granted him an unconditional pardon. One of the names appended to the petitions in Webb's behalf was that of Horace Greeley. Years afterwards the two men became involved in a war of words, and Webb made biting reference in the *Courier and Inquirer* to the dress usually worn by Greeley, asserting that he appeared on Broadway in uncouth garb merely to arrest the attention of the multitude. The next morning the *Tribune* contained an elaborate reply, going over Webb's article point by point. The last subject taken up by Greeley was Webb's reference to his dress. " As to our personal appearance," he said, " it does seem time that we should say something to stay the flood of nonsense with which the town must by this time be nauseated." He then went on to tell how he came to New York City, and worked as a journeyman printer ten or a dozen years before, with scarcely a dollar in his pocket, and how he had toiled until he had become the conductor of a leading journal of the country. Greeley closed his rejoinder by a reference to his efforts to secure Webb's pardon. It was most untrue, he asserted, that he ever affected eccentricity, "and certainly no costume he ever appeared in would create such a sensation as that Webb would have worn but for the clemency of Governor Seward. Heaven grant our assailant may never hang with such weight on another Whig executive. We drop him!"

It was said at the time that Webb laughed among the loudest at this keen retort of Greeley. Webb's connection with New York journalism lasted from 1827 until 1860, when he gave up the *Courier and Inquirer,* and that veteran newspaper was consolidated with the newly founded *World.* James Gordon Bennett was for several years a reporter on the *Courier and Inquirer,* and the account-book still exists in which the founder of the *Herald* was wont to sign a receipt for his salary of eight dollars a week.

Wall Street also has its memories for the lover of books and bookmen. A stroll along its paves recalls the people of Warner's "Golden House" and of Crawford's novels of New York life, of the hero of Janvier's "At the Casa Napoleon," and of the sturdy folk of an earlier time who keep one another company in Mrs. Barr's "The Bow of Orange Ribbon." Washington Irving, as we know, had his office in Wall Street during his brief excursion into the law, and here planned and partially executed his "Knickerbocker's History of New York." Halleck, Stoddard, and Stedman in later days have been numbered among the street's seekers after gold. Wiley the publisher long had his store in Wall Street, a favorite resort for Cooper, Paulding, and other of our early authors; and near its foot during the same period was the printing-office of Samuel Woodworth, who played many parts in his time but is now remembered only as the author of "The Old Oaken Bucket," such power has a homely ballad to win and hold the hearts of men.

V

Around City Hall Park

WHAT the Common is to Boston, City Hall Park is to New York. Known first as the Vlacte or Flat, later as the Commons, then as the Fields, and finally by its present name, it has been linked with every phase of the city's life and growth. Used as a cattle-walk when the palisades on the line of Wall Street marked the northern limits of the town, it became under the generous terms of the Dongan charter a part of the common lands vested in the city, and, thus set apart for public use, it remained for a century and a half the favorite meeting-place of the people on all occasions of public interest. There on the opening day of November, 1765, was held the first popular assembly in opposition to the Stamp Act; there the people gathered again and again during the stormy months that preceded its repeal; and there on June 4, 1766, they met to celebrate their victory with the potential aid of a roasted ox, washed down with "a hogshead of rum punch and twenty-five barrels of ale."

The flag-staff set up in the Commons on this joyous occasion became, as we know, a rallying-point for the patriot party and a bone of continuing contention between the royal soldiery and the Sons of Liberty, who had their head-quarters first at Montagnie's Tavern, No. 252 Broadway, and later at Hampton Hall, on the site of the St. Paul Building. Four times was the liberty-pole cut down by the soldiers and replaced by its vigilant defenders, one of these affairs having issue in the battle of Golden Hill and the first bloodshed of the Revolution. Parliament, meanwhile, had answered colonial defiance of the duty on tea with the passage of the Boston Port Act, and on July 6, 1774, New York again voiced its opposition to royal aggression in a great meeting held on the Commons, a meeting made doubly memorable by the maiden speech of Alexander Hamilton, then a seventeen-year-old student in King's College. History thereafter moved with hasting feet, and two years and three days later the Declaration of Independence was read to the patriot troops paraded on the Commons, with Washington and his staff at their head. Then came the British occupation and the thrall which made New York one of the heaviest sufferers for the cause of freedom.

Before the Revolution the city's first substantial buildings for charities and corrections had been erected in the Fields, as the Commons had now come to be known. The first of these was a poor-house, which stood from 1736 to 1797 about on the site of the present City Hall. Between 1756 and 1764 a jail was built on a line with and to the east of the almshouse, and the whipping-post, stocks, cage, and pillory were brought from Wall Street and set up in front of it, while the gallows, put to frequent use under the harsh laws then existing, stood a little retired in its rear. Finally, about 1775, the Bridewell—paid for by a lottery in which the city bought a thousand tickets—was built between the almshouse and Broadway, and continued to serve as a prison until 1838, when it was torn down and its stones used in the construction of the Tombs. All of these structures were of graystone, and the jail was surmounted by a tower, which later became a famous outlook for fires.

Both the jail and the Bridewell were used as patriot prisons during the Revolution. Provost-Marshal Cunningham of sinister memory had his head-quarters in the former building, occupying the room to the right of the entrance, and so gave to it the name of the Provost, or the Provost Jail. It is needless now to speak of the cruelties to which he subjected the Americans committed to his care, but a single incident of those dark times may well find a place in this chronicle. One of the prisoners in the Provost was a member of Washington's life-guard, who, having volunteered for service as a spy, was arrested while apparently deserting from the British army, and forthwith condemned to death. The night fixed for his execution, Cunningham, with a file of soldiers and a negro hangman, set out for the gallows in the neighborhood of City Hall Place. The bodies of two men hanged the previous night were swinging on the gallows, and the negro, to clear the way for his new task, drew his knife and began cutting the ropes.

Then the unexpected befell. A patriot trooper, bent upon saving his comrade's life, had stolen within the enemy's lines under cover of the night, and for an hour had been hiding in the grave already opened to receive the deserter. The ropes severed by the negro, the bodies fell to earth, and one slid into the grave where lay the patriot soldier; but the latter made no sign, for quick wit told him that chance had thrown in his way an opportunity to rescue his friend. The condemned man begged five minutes for prayer. Three were granted him. He knelt down, and heard a familiar voice tell him to turn his back to the grave when he had spent his three minutes, and his bonds would be cut. The prisoner obeyed this whispered command, and with limbs unfettered darted away into the darkness just as the hangman stepped forward to adjust the noose. Then uprose from the grave the "ghost" of the dead man whose body a few moments before had fallen into it, and provost, guard, and hangman fled in white terror from the spot. Five minutes later rescuer and rescued were making their way over Lispenard's Meadows and down to the river's edge, whence a boat, provided for the purpose, carried them in safety to the Jersey shore. The following day there were two new lieutenants in Washington's life-guard, and Cunningham was still wondering as to how his quarry had escaped him.

The Revolution ended, the Provost became a place of detention for debtors; and how numerous was its new class of tenants is shown by the fact that between January and December of the year 1788 nearly twelve hundred residents of the town, one in every twenty of its male population went to jail for debt. This condition of affairs, however, led to the founding of the Society for the Relief of Distressed Debtors, and through the efforts of that body to the passage of an act which limited imprisonment for debts of ten pounds or less to thirty days and for larger amounts to three months, provided the debtor made oath that he had no property wherewith to pay his debts. The Provost after that had fewer lodgers, and these had dwindled to less than twoscore when in 1817 a second modification of the law granted immunity to all confined for sums not exceeding twenty-five dollars. Twelve years later, all need for a debtor's prison as a separate institution having disappeared, and there being demand for a fire-proof building in which to house the city records, the common council decided to reconstruct the Provost and devote it to this purpose. It was accordingly cut down a story and encased in new outer walls; and when in 1832 the offices of the register, the comptroller, and the surrogate were housed together within them, boastful citizens pointed out the transformed jail as the most beautiful structure on Manhattan Island. This estimate will not be questioned by trained observers of a later time, for the Hall of Records, since 1870 tenanted only by the register, is patterned upon that wonder of the ancient world, the temple of Diana of Ephesus, and so bears witness to the grace and simple elegance of Chersiphron's master-piece.

The Fields laid the grounds for its present name in 1785, when it was enclosed with a post-and-rail fence, which soon gave way to one of wooden palings, and this in 1816 to an iron railing "set up with due ceremony and public commemoration of the event." The old almshouse had the while been torn down to furnish a site for the present City Hall, and a new one erected at the north end of the park. When the paupers were transferred to Bellevue in 1812, this second building was devoted to various undertakings of a public character, and under the name of the New York Institution at divers periods furnished quarters for the New York Historical Society, the Academy of Arts, the Lyceum of Natural History, and Scudder's Museum. There in 1819 was organized the city's first bank for savings, whose present home is at the corner of Fourth Avenue and Twenty-second Street, and there also during the same decade the Deaf and Dumb Institute, now located on Washington Heights, opened its first school with four pupils. The building was demolished a few years before the Civil War, and its site is now occupied by the county court-house. And finally, City Hall Park was given its present size and shape by the erection of the granite building at its southern end which since 1875 has furnished a home for the city post-office, although it is doubtful if a later generation would have allowed it to be curtailed for an even worthier purpose.

Broadway from Vesey to Duane Street and facing the Commons was first surveyed under the name of Great George Street in 1760, but was not paved or otherwise improved until after the Revolution. West of it lay the Church Farm, which about the same time was divided into streets and blocks as far north as Duane Street. The old house attached to this farm stood on the site of the Astor House, and in its last days was known as the Drovers' Inn. There had been a rope-walk between Barclay and Robinson Streets (now Park Place) as early as 1719, and for many years after 1760 the most conspicuous features of this part of Broadway were a number of public gardens, the best remembered that of Abraham Montagnie, near the corner of Murray Street. There, as we know, the Sons of

Liberty for a time had their head-quarters. Montagnie, however, was a landlord before he was patriot, and his willingness when opportunity offered to let his rooms to the royalist faction finally caused the Liberty Boys to remove in hot dudgeon to Hampden Hall, opposite the lower end of the Fields. Montagnie continued in business until after the Revolution, and was the last to own and display the famous King's Arms sign, which had passed through various hands and hung over taverns in different parts of the town. His garden became later the site for a building called the Parthenon, which in 1825 was occupied as a museum by Reuben Peale, forerunner of the more noted Barnum.

Great George Street in 1794 became a part of Broadway, and, paved and planted with trees, soon developed into a favorite place of residence. Edward Livingston, when mayor of the city, lived at No. 223 Broadway, with Rufus King and Aaron Burr for neighbors, while later residents of this part of the street were John Jacob Astor and Jacob Lydig. Philip Hone for many years had his home at No. 235 Broadway, and between Chambers and Reade Streets was the fine residence of Matthias Bruen, one of the merchant princes of his time. The Bruen mansion, however, was elbowed by humble neighbors, and in one of these, a low and narrow structure with gable end to the street, Alexander T. Stewart began the dry-goods business in New York. Stewart had come from Ireland two years before, and found a place as teacher in a school in Roosevelt Street near Pearl. While thus employed a young man with whom he had become intimate applied to him for money wherewith to start a dry-goods store. He advanced the greater part of the modest sum he had brought to America, and a small store was stocked, but through an unforeseen circumstance his friend, after the preparations had been made, was unable to begin business.

Stewart, in order that the money he had invested might not be lost, resolved to carry on the business himself. He went back to Ireland, converted into cash the estate his father had left him, bought a stock of Belfast laces, and returned to New York to open his store. The capital invested was about three thousand dollars, and in the *Daily Advertiser* of September 2, 1825, appeared a card announcing that A. T. Stewart offered for sale, at No. 283 Broadway, "a general assortment of fresh and seasonable dry goods." His shop had only twelve feet front. He lived over it, and for a time was his own errand-boy, porter, book-keeper, and salesman. His progress was not brilliant at the outset, and he owed the assurance of success to an accident that would have brought most men to despair: A note came due which he was not able to pay, and an extension of time was refused him. But the pluck and energy which were the heritage of his Scotch-Irish ancestry helped him to master this crisis in his fortunes. Instead of applying to friends for aid, he marked every article in his store below the wholesale price, and flooded the town with handbills, telling what he had and what he proposed to sell. The following morning his shop was crowded with folk seeking bargains, and before the week was ended he had sold every article in it for cash. When he counted his receipts he found he had money with which to pay the note that was pressing him, and a handsome balance for the purchase of a new stock of goods.

Learning wisdom from experience, Stewart resolved to purchase no more on credit, and this rule was never broken during the remainder of his business career. What was equally essential to his success, those who bought at his sale found when they examined their purchases that instead of being cheated they had really got bargains; and after that his store could boast a growing army of patrons. He removed at the end of a year to larger quarters at No. 262 Broadway, and not long afterwards he again transferred his stock to No. 257 Broadway. Fourteen years later his multiplying trade and capital enabled him to build a large marble store at Broadway and Chambers Street, on the site of Washington Hall. His business, however, soon outgrew these spacious quarters, and in 1862 he leased the block bounded by Ninth and Tenth Streets, Broadway and Fourth Avenue, and erected thereon what long remained the largest retail store in the world. Its owner had a genius for organization; the right man was always put in the right place; and when he died in 1875 he left to his heirs a fortune of many millions.

The sequel of Stewart's career nevertheless stamped it a splendid failure,—a failure that had in it all the elements of a Greek tragedy. He left no son to take up the work of the father, and dry-rot spread through the enterprises he had set in motion, for those who succeeded him had thought more of his money than his purposes. Time came when even the great house at Ninth

Street, which he had designed to be his most enduring monument, closed its doors, "forced to the wall by importunate small-money creditors on a stringent market." To-day it bears another name, and that of its founder is swiftly fading from the minds of men.

In the days when Stewart first occupied his marble building at the corner of Chambers Street, the Irving House, a fashionable hostelry, held the opposite corner of Broadway. There in a yet earlier time John C. Colt had his office, and there he murdered Samuel Adams, a printer in his employ. The two men quarrelled over a question of money, and Colt, in the white heat of passion, beat Adams to death with a hammer. Then the murderer, appalled by his crime, sought to hide the evidences of it. He packed the body of his victim in a box, marked it for New Orleans and shipped it by a vessel lying at the foot of Maiden Lane. The ship did not sail as advertised, and when rewards were offered for information regarding the whereabouts of Adams, a cartman reported to the authorities that he had taken a box from the Chambers Street building to a packet lying in the East River. Thereupon the box was fished from the bottom of the hold, and disclosure of its contents led to the arrest of

Colt, whose subsequent trial, despite the efforts of able counsel, ended in a verdict of murder and a sentence to the gallows. Colt's friends and counsel made a strenuous fight for him after conviction, but appeals proved fruitless. The morning he was to die he was married in his cell to the sweetheart who had clung to him even in the shadow of death. The bride was allowed to have an hour with her husband, and then he asked to be left alone until the time of his execution. When the warden, a little later, went to warn him to be in readiness, he found Colt dead by his own hand,—the blade of a bowie knife thrust to the hilt through his heart.

Park Row, formerly Chatham Street and once part of the Bowery, follows from Ann Street to Chatham Square the line of the post-road to Boston, and is rich in memories of the olden days. Through it Stuyvesant rode to reach his bouwery, Leisler and Milborne were hanged beside it, and over it in colony times moved all of the travel between New York and New England. The first post established in America passed through this road, and down it dashed the courier with the news of Concord and Lexington. The *Tribune* Building occupies the whilom site of Martling's Tavern, where the Tammany Society grew into lusty youth and made ready to build the hall on the site of the *Sun* Building, whence it removed in 1867 to its present headquarters in Fourteenth Street, while fourscore years ago the portion of Park Row lying between Ann and Spruce Streets was almost entirely occupied by the Park Theatre and by the Brick Church, which stood on the site of the *Times* and Potter Buildings.

The "Brick Meeting," as it was more familiarly known, was an off-shoot of the Presbyterian Church in Wall Street, and its first pastor was Dr. John Rodgers, a man of fervent piety and ardent patriotism, who during the Revolution served as a brigade chaplain in Washington's army. Tradition has it that he was a man of "the most majestic dignity, and in manners so formal that the last thing he and his wife always did before retiring for the night was to salute each other with a bow and courtesy." Rodgers was succeeded by Dr. Gardner Spring, a forceful preacher and prolific maker of books, who held the pulpit for sixty-two years. The Brick Meeting served as a place of worship from 1767 to 1856, when it was torn down and the church at Fifth Avenue and Thirty-seventh Street built by the congregation. The parent structure was flanked by a burial-ground, and the Potter Building hides the graves of hundreds who once worshipped within its walls.

A similar fate long since overtook St. George's Chapel, which stood in other days at the near-by corner of Beekman and Cliff Streets. This famous church, built and opened in 1752, was a daughter of Trinity, and it counted among its members during the later colonial period the Schuylers, Livingstons, Beekmans, Van Rensselaers, and Courtlandts. It was rebuilt after its destruction by fire in 1814, and was occupied until 1841, when it was demolished and its congregation removed to the present church in Rutherford Place near Stuyvesant Square. St. George's also had its graveyard dotted with tombstones, but this was sold with the rest of the property, and now a warehouse covers the ground once devoted to church and burial-garth.

Time and change have dealt more kindly with the site of the first Methodist Church in New York. It was in 1760 that a band of Irish emigrants, converted by his preaching, brought the faith of John Wesley to America. One of them was Philip Embury, a carpenter, who worked at his trade on week-days and on Sundays preached to his fellows, first in a private house on what is now Park Place, and later in a rigging loft at No. 120 William Street, then known as Horse and Cart Lane. While quartered in this building the Methodists leased a plot of ground on the south side of John Street, between Nassau and William, and on it built a chapel which they named after Wesley. Embury worked as a carpenter on the building, and when it was finished preached the dedication sermon. Wesley Chapel, a low stone building without a steeple, was replaced in 1817 by a large granite church, but in 1841 the second structure was in turn demolished for the erection of the present building, Nos. 44-46 John Street. No landmark in the city attracts a greater number of reverent visitors, and with reason, for the sect which in 1760 numbered but six persons in the congregation and gathered those in a small room, is now the largest Protestant denomination in America, having six millions of members, and sustaining thousands of churches, schools, and colleges.

The corner of Spruce and Nassau Streets became the home of the *Tribune* in 1842, and there Horace Greeley did the work which won him enduring fame. "Our later Franklin," as Whittier in one of his poems called him, Greeley was in a peculiar sense the *Tribune,* nor did he himself ever lose sight of that fact. A Whig politician of importance in one of the rural districts of the State made the journey to New York and found his way to the *Tribune* office. There he first accosted Thomas McElrath, the partner of Greeley, who asked him if he would like to look over the establishment. The caller said that was the object of his visit, and the publisher proceeded to show him the presses, the engines, the mailing department and the counting-room. "Now," said McElrath, with a deep breath of satisfaction, "you have seen the *Tribune,*" and he left him to recover from his astonishment. But the visitor, still unsatisfied, concluded to go up-stairs and see Greeley. Entering the editor's room unannounced, he greeted his Whig compatriot with hearty phrase and told him he had come from his country-home to see the *Tribune.* Greeley turned from the desk, at whose level he kept his chin when engaged in writing, and gave his visitor cordial welcome. After exchanges of personal and party sentiment, the editor broke out with, "So, you've come to see the *Tribune,* have you?" Snatching up the old white hat always conveniently at hand, he clapped it on his head, and out of the mouth of the child's face beneath came the answer, "There! you see the *Tribune* inside this hat!"

Rank and station had no weight with Greeley. He valued men not for what they were, but for what they did; and he was accessible at all times to the humblest and lowliest of the land. Visitors there were, however, who could not count upon a cordial welcome. Half a dozen Republicans from the interior of the State came to the city, and under the guidance of a well-known member of the party went to the office of the *Tribune* to give its chief a bit of wholesome advice. Greeley, who divined their object, continued his writing until the spokesman had several times introduced the country politicians with the words, "Here are a number of influential Republicans, Mr. Greeley, who would like to talk to you about certain matters of much importance to the party." Still no reply from the busy man at the desk. Once more, "Mr. Greeley, these gentlemen have great influence in the State; they are——" "A set of confounded asses. I know that," broke in the editor, without looking up. "They are wasting their time, and trying to waste mine, by coming here." This rebuff ended the interview. The politicians retreated in confusion, and the editor went on with his work.

The granite building of the *Staats-Zeitung,* which faces City Hall Park from what was once known as Tryon Row, is a monument to the genius and energy of an uncommon woman. Jacob Uhl, a printer, came to this country from Bavaria, and for eight years worked as a journeyman, being assisted in his struggles by the wife he had married before departing from the fatherland. Then, in 1844, the young German and his helpmeet bought a printing-outfit and set up for themselves at No. 11 Frankfort Street. German printers were few, and the job-printing office flourished from the start. Near the Uhls was the office of the *Staats-Zeitung,* a struggling German newspaper. Mrs. Uhl persuaded her husband to buy it, and in a short time they enlarged the sheet and improved its appearance. A little later, as German emigration was rapidly increasing, Mrs. Uhl proposed to turn it into a daily, and the husband, believing in his wife's foresight, put her idea into practice. He died in 1852, when the *Staats-Zeitung* was climbing into assured success.

Mrs. Uhl after her husband's death became chief editor of the newspaper, which expanded under her energetic and tactful management until it occupied two great buildings in Chatham Row. Following her marriage to Oswald Ottendorfer in 1859, she resigned the chief editorship to her husband; but she continued to take an active part in the business management, and until the end of her days no important step in the course of the paper was ever determined upon without her consent. Moreover, she only cared for money in order to make beneficent use of it, and in her later years gave more than a million dollars to wise and helpful charities. She died in 1884, and, with a funeral procession such as rarely attends the obsequies of a private citizen, was laid to rest in Greenwood Cemetery. The *Staats-Zeitung,* had it not been for her, would never have survived its infancy, still less attained its present power and prestige.

Chambers Street east of Broadway runs through ground that in the early days of the town was used as a burial-place for negroes, but for many an aging man it recalls delightful memories of the playhouse which long occupied the site of the American News Company's Building. This theatre was originally called Palmo's Opera-House, and in the early forties a brave but futile attempt was there made to give Italian opera a permanent home. The house was then leased to William E. Burton, who made it from 1848 to 1856 the theatre best beloved by patrons of comedy. Burton held first rank among the comic actors of his time, being equally happy as Toodles, as Falstaff, as Sir Toby Belch, as Bottom, and as Caliban; and he gathered about him in Chambers Street a company of players hardly less gifted than himself, a company which included John Brougham and James H. Stoddart, and offered admirable training to a score of younger players. Maggie Mitchell made her first appearance with the Burton company, and Frank Chanfrau had with it his first engagement as a professional actor.

A stone's throw from the scene of Burton's triumphs one comes at Nos. 195-197 Park Row upon the site of another famous playhouse of the middle years of the last century,—the Chatham Theatre, opened to the public in 1839, and known in its later days as the New National. Thomas Flynn, friend and comrade of the elder Booth, was the first manager of this house, and among the players who began their career on its boards were Fanny Herring, Mrs. D. P. Bowers, and the latter's sister, Mrs. Conway. Mr. and Mrs. William J. Florence first appeared as stars at this theatre, and there in 1859 Ada Isaacs Menken made her New York début, as George L. Fox had done at an earlier time. There, too, Chanfrau won fame in the character of Mose the fireman, Forrest first played Othello in New York, and the elder Adams proved his genius and power as an actor. Yet another noteworthy incident in the history of this house was the first New York production, in 1852, of "Uncle Tom's Cabin." The New National closed its doors in 1861, and the building, with few tokens of its early history remaining, is now used as a store.

City Hall Park and the streets adjacent to it have also their store of literary associations. The office of the *Home Journal,* which had Willis and Morris for its editors, was long at No. 107 Fulton Street, and Ray Palmer was a teacher in a private school only a few doors removed when he composed "My Faith looks up to Thee." Horace Greeley once lived and Frederick S. Cozzens had his office in Vesey Street, while on Park Row were the shop of David Longworth, the publisher of "Salmagundi," and the wine-cellar of Edward Windust, a favorite resort of the authors, actors, and artists who flourished in the opening years of the last century. William Dunlap, painter, historian, and dramatist by turns, and nothing long, abode for many years upon the second block of Beekman Street, and must often have crossed the park to visit Dr. John W. Francis, who had his office and residence in Chambers Street. In a building now gone from No. 9 Spruce Street were the office of the *Saturday Press,* edited by Henry Clapp, and the New York head-quarters of the Brook Farm association, where Hawthorne, Ripley, Curtis, and Margaret Fuller frequently foregathered to chat about their literary and business experiences and to renew old friendships. Greeley began his New York career in a printing-office at No. 85 Chatham Street, and hard by in Duane Street was the house, now supplanted by stores, in which Woodworth lived when he wrote "The Old Oaken Bucket." Woodworth later had his home in Pearl Street near Elm, and there he died after long and wasting illness.

A store at No. 5 Barclay Street occupies the site of Frank's restaurant, once a favorite meeting-place of the wits of the town; at No. 10 Park Place George William Curtis, Parke Godwin, and Charles F. Briggs, better known as Harry Franco, conducted *Putnam's Magazine;* and in Murray Street near to Broadway was the first city home of Bayard Taylor, who there had

Charles Fenno Hoffman for a fellow-lodger. And to recall one other literary wraith, Broadway in the neighborhood of City Hall Park was the place most frequented by McDonald Clarke, the hapless hero of Halleck's "Discarded," and himself the author of much tender and graceful verse. Clarke first appeared in New York when a youth of twenty-one, and he remained until his death a melancholy and unmistakable figure in the life of the town,—made so by his poetic genius, his sharp wit, and the vagaries of an unbalanced mind. Broadway was his chosen haunt, and for a score of years his tall form, in blue coat and cloth cap, was one of the familiar objects of that thoroughfare. No one knew aught of his antecedents or of his means of support, aside from the sale of his books of verse, but the sequel proved that he was often in need both of food and lodging. On a stormy night in March, 1842, a policeman came upon him wandering about the streets, destitute and demented, and took him to the city prison for warmth and shelter. The following morning he was found dead, having drowned himself in his cell. Friends provided a tomb and burial, and he sleeps now in the poet's mound on the margin of Sylvan Lake in Greenwood.

SECTION TWO

THE COMMON
TO
LOVE LANE

VI

Broadway above the Common

THE middle Broadway of the present holds few visible tokens of the thoroughfare of seventy years ago. Then it was planted with trees from Leonard Street to Astor Place, and flanked above Canal Street with the homes of men of means who still clung to it as a place of residence. The sloping grounds of the New York Hospital, shaded by elms that overtopped the highest houses, were on the west side of the street, beginning at Duane and extending more than two-thirds of the block. Masonic Hall was on the opposite side of the way, covering the site of the stores now known as Nos. 314 and

316 Broadway, and on the same side, between Pearl and Worth Streets, stood the Broadway Theatre, for a dozen years after 1847 the playhouse most affected by fashion.

There Edwin Forrest played his annual engagements, the New York public first saw "Monte Cristo," with young Lester Wallack as Dantes, and Charles W. Couldock began his career in America in the title-rôle of "The Stranger," with Charlotte Cushman, fresh from her European triumphs, as Mrs. Haller. The play of "Ingomar" had its first American production at the Broadway; upon its stage Lola Montez, an Irish girl masquerading under a Spanish name, charmed the town for a day, only to die a few years later in poverty and obscurity; while Jean Davenport, afterwards Mrs. Lander, here introduced Camille to the American public, and also captivated them with her performance of Peg Woffington in "Masks and Faces." The theatre closed its doors in 1859, after a splendid revival of "Antony and Cleopatra," with Madame Ponisi as Cleopatra, counted by many the best portrayal of that character ever seen in America. An earlier Broadway Theatre stood from 1837 to 1846 near the corner of Walker Street; and at the Anthony Street Theatre, situated in what is now Worth Street, just west of Broadway, Edmund Kean made his first appearance in America. There also the play of "Virginius" was first seen in New York. This playhouse was burned in 1824, after a career of a decade, and later Christ Church was built on its site, only to make way for business houses.

The Broadway Tabernacle for many years occupied a portion of the block between Worth Street and Catherine Lane, its walls echoing the appeals of the champions of the slave; between Catherine Lane and Leonard Street long stood the building of the Society Library, which afterwards furnished a home for the publishing-house of the Appletons; and on the opposite side of the next block in the early decades of the last century flourished an institution held in grateful memory by aged men who still keep their spirits young,—John Contoit's New York Garden. "Its plain wooden entrance," we are told by one who knew its charms at first hand, "was overshadowed by trees, and inside were shady nooks, dimly lit by colored lanterns, where the young woman of the period found it pleasant to sip her cream and listen to the compliments of the young man of the times. Many a match was made in these old gardens, which to-day would seem to the eye but the acme of rural simplicity, but to the older city offered all that was enjoyable of a moonlight night on Manhattan."

Crossing Canal Street, spanned in other days by a stone bridge, one finds a business structure covering at No. 442 Broadway, between Howard and Grand Streets, the site of the Olympic, a tiny box of a theatre, where, after 1839, William Mitchell reigned as king of burlesque actors. Mitchell was a born child of Momus, gifted with wonderful mimic powers, and no player of note escaped his trenchant burlesque. His caricatures of Kean, Forrest, and the elder Booth were marvels of grotesque imitation; but one of his earliest and most popular representations was based upon the Tarantula of Fanny Elssler, whose dancing was then the talk of the town. "We shall long remember," writes Dr. Northall, "the comic humor with which he burlesqued the charming and graceful Fanny. The manner of his exit from the stage was irresistibly comic, and the serious care with which he guided himself to the side scenes to secure a passage for his tremendous bustle was very funny." Mitchell's reign—his company included Mary Taylor, prettiest and jolliest of soubrettes—came to an end in 1849, but gray-beards there are who

BROADWAY IN 1840, BETWEEN HOWARD AND GRAND STREETS

declare that for genuine fun New York has had no successor to the little Olympic.

The same gray-beards grow eloquent when mention is made of Christy's minstrels, who in 1846 began their metropolitan career at the hall of the Mechanics' Society, No. 472 Broadway. The Christys brought to perfection the style of negro minstrelsy long so popular, and their career in Broadway was a prosperous and merry one. They remained at Mechanics' Hall until the summer of 1854, when George Christy, the leader and founder of the company, retired from business. Three years later Bryant's minstrels occupied the old hall, and held sway there until in 1868 it was destroyed by fire, never to be rebuilt for amusement purposes.

Minstrelsy, however, found more than one other home in Broadway. Bryant's company was at No. 730 Broadway in 1869; Wood's minstrels were lodged for a time at No. 514 Broadway; and for seven years following 1865 the San Francisco minstrels were at No. 585 Broadway. David Wambold and Charles Backus were the bright particular stars of the company last named, and it does not need a gray-beard to recall the gibes, the gambols, the songs, and the flashes of merriment that made an evening at

"585" a source of unalloyed delight. There came upon the minstrel stage in his day no sweeter singer than Wambold, while Backus's vein of rich and fetching humor was a never-failing one. They made the world happier and brighter by their presence, and when they died they left no successors.

A warehouse at No. 485 Broadway, near the southwest corner of Broome Street, covers the site of another playhouse of the old days. There in 1850 John Brougham opened his Lyceum which two years later became Wallack's Lyceum Theatre. James W. Wallack, first of his line in America, was one of the most gifted of comedians in the higher walk, and he drew about him at the "first Wallack's" a company that included among others John Lester (later famous as Lester Wallack), John Brougham, William Rufus Blake, the elder George Holland, Edward A. Sothern, William R. Floyd, Mrs. John Wood, Mrs. John Hoey, Mary Gannon, and Mrs. Vernon. Laura Keene made at this house her first appearance in America, and there Matilda Heron, a woman of astonishing, if uneven, genius, enjoyed a meteoric career in "Camille." All the old comedies were yearly produced on its boards, along with many new ones, including

" Love and Money," " London Assurance," and " Old Heads and Young Hearts," probably the best of Dion Boucicault's works.

The Broadway and Broome Street Wallack's lasted until 1861, when the company was transferred to a new and more spacious theatre at the northeast corner of Broadway and Thirteenth Street. The elder Wallack died in 1864, and Lester Wallack, who had taken his father's place in popular favor, inherited the theatre. The father's good luck attended the son, and for the better part of twenty years the " second Wallack's," held first place among American theatres. During that period E. L. Davenport, John Gilbert, Mark Smith, Charles Fisher, John Sefton, Charles Parsloe, Charles Wyndham, Henry J. Montague, Harry Becket, Harry Edwards, Owen Marlowe, Madeline Henriques, Fanny Morant, Ione Burke, Ada Dyas, Effie Germon, Rose Coghlan, Mrs. Winter, and Madame Ponisi, players already famous or destined to achieve distinction, were among the members of the company. Many of the plays in which these actors appeared linger lovingly in the memory of old theatre-goers,—" Rosedale," " Ours," " School," " Diplomacy," and Boucicault's " Colleen Bawn" and the " Shaugraun," in which its author acted the title-rôle. Lester Wallack gave up the house at Thirteenth Street in 1881 and moved to the theatre at Thirtieth Street and Broadway which still bears his name. The Thirteenth Street house, after a brief interlude, was renamed the Star, and became for a time a favorite theatre for star actors. Henry Irving and Ellen Terry made their first American appearance there, and among others who played in it were Edwin Booth, Wilson Barrett, Helena Modjeska, and Sarah Bernhardt. Later still it became the home of melodramas produced with little or no regard for histrionic art, and in 1901 was demolished to make way for an office-building. When the Wallack company left it, the Broadway and Broome Street house became the third Broadway Theatre, and until its demolition in 1869 was given up to stars. There Charles Kean made his last American appearance and Julia Dean took her farewell of the stage.

Old St. Thomas's, built in 1823 at the corner of Broadway and Houston Street, was long since replaced by stores, and a like fate has overtaken the church on the opposite side of the way where Dr. Edwin H. Chapin, radical and impassioned, preached for many years to great congregations. Dr. Chapin's church was situated at

No. 548 Broadway, and within its walls, in the fall of 1852, William M. Thackeray delivered his first lectures upon the English humorists to audiences who knew their enjoyment to be the highest kind of literary pleasure. Wherever the novelist went in America he was welcomed in the most cordial manner, and everywhere he left behind him enduring memories of his kindliness and sturdy simplicity. Just before he sailed upon his return to England he gave a dinner to repay many courtesies, and assembled twenty or thirty guests of distinction. " Thackeray was in high spirits," writes George William Curtis, " and when the cigars were lighted he said there should be no speech-making, but that everybody, according to the old rule of festivity, should sing a song or tell a story. James Wallack was one of the guests, and with a kind of shyness, which was unexpected but very agreeable in a veteran actor, he pleaded earnestly that he could not sing and knew no stories. But with friendly persistence, which yet was not immoderate, Thackeray declared that no excuse could be allowed, because it would be a manifest injustice to every other modest man at the table and would put a summary end to the hilarity. 'Now, Wallack,' he continued, 'we all know you to be a truthful man. You can, of course, since you say so, neither sing a song nor tell a story. But I tell you what you can do better than any living man,—you can give us the great scene from "The Rent Day."' There was a burst of enthusiastic agreement, and old Wallack, smiling and yielding, still sitting at the table in his evening dress, proceeded in a most effective and touching recitation of one of his most famous parts. No enjoyment of it was greater and no applause sincerer than those of Thackeray, who presently sang his 'Little Billie' with infinite gusto."

If Thackeray had been minded to make a book out of his American experiences he abandoned it at starting. "As for writing about this country," runs one of his letters to an old friend in England, "about the friends I have found here, and who are helping me to procure independence for my children, if I cut jokes against them, may I choke on the instant. If I can say anything to show that my name is really Makepeace, and to increase the source of love between the two countries, then, please God, I will. The laugh dies out as we get old, you see, but the love and the truth don't, praised be God! and I begin to think of the responsibilities of this pen now writing to you with a feeling of no small awe. The first name I heard in the railroad was my own by a pretty child selling books. So, here it is after fifteen years, think I, here's the fame they talk about. My impression, though, was one of awe and humility rather than exultation, and to pray God I might keep honest and tell the truth always."

And so, instead of a stereotyped record of travel, Thackeray gave us that delightful book "The Virginians," in part the result of his visit, and wrote for use on a second tour in America his illuminating lectures on the four Georges. This second tour, begun in the fall of 1855, was also a prosperous one, and though often ill, the lecturer was happy, and wrote home cheery letters, some of which have lately been given to the world by his daughter. Wherever he went he was again received with the utmost kindness, and great was his delight when told by Dr. Kane, just returned from the Arctic, that he had seen one of his seamen crouched over a book for hours, and behold it was "Pendennis." One amusing adventure quoted by Mrs. Ritchie recalls Mr. Pickwick's most terrifying experience. "Had a pleasant dinner with a party at Delmonico's," wrote the novelist. "Came home late and had an awful escape,—I tremble when

I think of it. Took my key at the bar, entered my apartment, began to pull off my boots, etc., etc., when a sweet female voice from the room within exclaimed, 'George!' I had gone into the second-floor room instead of the third. I gathered my raiment together and dashed out of the premises."

The paves of middle Broadway echo the footfalls of other authors, most of whom have been withdrawn "to where beyond these voices there is peace." Cooper the novelist lived for several years on the east side of Broadway above Prince Street, when just across the way was the home of John Jacob Astor, where Irving wrote a portion of his "Life of Washington." Julia Ward Howe was born and passed her girlhood in a house now gone from one of the Broadway corners of Bond Street, while the basement of the building No. 653 Broadway, a few doors above Bleecker, was forty-odd years ago Charles Pfaff's beer-cellar, the haunt of the cleverest of New York's literary Bohemians.

Henry Clapp, a brilliant but desultory writer who had lived by his wits in nearly every part of the globe, was the king of this new-world Bohemia. Lounging into Pfaff's place one day in 1856, in company with Fitz-James O'Brien, he was so delighted with the beer served him that he straightway sounded its praises among his comrades, who thereupon made Pfaff's their favorite resort. A table, about which some thirty could find seats, was reserved for their use, and around it gathered almost nightly for several years such men as Clapp, O'Brien, Walt Whitman, George Arnold, Edwin Wilkins, Charles Dawson Shanly, and Charles Farrar Browne, more familiarly known as Artemus Ward. Nearly all of the coterie were writers for the *Saturday Press,* a weekly paper edited by Clapp, or for *Vanity Fair,* a comic journal conducted by Ward. Walt Whitman, with slouch hat and suit of gray, red shirt open at the neck, and long flowing hair, was the most picturesque and striking figure of the group. His "Leaves of Grass" was then fresh from the press, and every one who read flocked to Pfaff's of evenings to see the man whose verses sang the praises of their author and the lusts of the flesh in the same breath.

All of the little band had ability, and many of them genius; but strong drink and late hours were not the elements from which to expect enduring success, and soon the young men who drank so deeply and faced the world so joyously discovered their mistake. Then the failure of the journals conducted by Clapp and Ward dissolved the chief links that held them together, and the Civil War scattered them far and wide. O'Brien, a handsome Irishman, who wrote with equal ease stirring virile poems or weirdly powerful stories, inferior only to those of Poe, enlisted as a volunteer in defence of the Union, and fell bravely fighting at Bloomery Gap. Wilkins, one of the best dramatic critics ever associated with the New York press, died in the early sixties, and so did Arnold, whose tender and graceful verse still finds admiring readers; while Ward's career ended in England before he was thirty, and when he should have been preparing to do his strongest and best work. Of the others whom time has taken, poor Clapp was himself one of the last to go. He died under the saddest circumstances on Blackwell's Island, and his funeral expenses were borne by men and women who admired his genius without joining in the excesses that hurried him to the grave.

Two other members of the "Pfaff crowd" demand a word,—Ada Clare and Jenny Danforth. The former was a Southern girl of birth and breeding, a cousin of the poet Paul Hayne, and had been carefully educated; but with the taste that seemed born in her for an unconventional life, she drifted to New York, where she became an occasional writer and actress, and the boon companion of the hale fellows who gathered about Pfaff's round table. She was a great beauty "and the embodiment of female Bohemianism. Seated at the table, with her mass of yellow hair shining above her head and her face flushed with excitement, she parried thrusts of wit as deftly as a swordsman would a foil, and her laugh rang the clearest when an unfortunate one was unhorsed in the shock of intellect." Ada Clare's last years were sorrowful ones. She outlived her beauty and most of her old companions to die of hydrophobia, the result of a bite of a pet dog. Jenny Danforth was also a witty and beautiful woman, the estranged wife, it was said, of a naval officer of high rank, but whose name was not Danforth. A clever writer, she lived for a few years a precarious but not wholly unhappy life, and then falling into misfortune and poverty, finally vanished without her old friends knowing precisely when or how it happened.

The corner of Broadway and Prince Street recalls memories of Niblo's Garden,—one of the last of the old New York theatres to succumb to the demands of trade. It was in 1828 that William Niblo started a series of concerts in connection with a coffee-house on this site. The following year he built a more pretentious concert-hall, and there in the summer of 1837 the Ravels, the pantomimists, appeared, not for the first time in this country, but for their most famous performances. They continued to play there at intervals for many years. Niblo's Garden became Niblo's Theatre in 1839, and with William Chippendale, an English actor, as stage-manager, had a prosperous career until 1846, when it was burned. During this period Edward L. Davenport made his first New York appearance at this house. It was rebuilt in 1849, and opened in 1850, with a play by Brougham. Eight-year-old Adelina Patti made her first appearance at Niblo's on December 3, 1851, and there her wonderful voice first attracted attention. Four years later came Rachel, the French actress, and after her Dion Boucicault and his wife Agnes Robertson gave numerous plays. There the "Black Crook" was given first in 1867, and the season of 1871 brought Lydia Thompson and her company. The theatre, owned after 1861 by Alexander T. Stewart and his estate, was burned again in 1872, but at once rebuilt, and thereafter devoted, in the main, to spectacle and melodrama, the first production of "Evangeline" in 1874 being one of the best remembered incidents in its later history. It finally closed its doors in 1894, and gave way to an office-building.

Business structures have also replaced the theatre at Nos. 622 and 624 Broadway, between Houston and Bleecker Streets, where for several years after 1856 Laura Keene and a company of gifted players gave delight to thousands. There the elder Sothern entered into his own as Lord Dundreary, while Miss Keene played in the "Sea of Ice" and the "Seven Sisters," and gained fortune and repute, speedily losing the one, but keeping the other even to the present day. This theatre became the Olympic in 1863, under the management of Mrs. John Wood, and later the passing home of "Humpty Dumpty," with George L. Fox, whose comic powers were of the first order, in the title-rôle. There also in 1870 Fox appeared for many weeks in his delightful travesty of Hamlet. This sterling player, the best Shakespearian comedian within the memory of living men, was last seen at Booth's Theatre in November, 1875,—"the saddest clown who ever chalked his face." Then, broken in spirit, he disappeared from public view to end his days in the starless gloom of a refuge for the insane. When Mrs. Wood managed the Olympic, Joseph Jefferson, at that time best known as a burlesque actor, was a member of her company, and there was first seen as Rip Van Winkle.

The National Academy of Design had its home for several years following 1849 at No. 663 Broadway, nearly opposite Bond Street. This association, the oldest of the city's art bodies, was organized in 1826 under the leadership of Samuel F. B. Morse, and the same year held its first exhibition in the second-story room of a house on the corner of Broadway and Reade Street. Its second exhibition was held in the third story of the building in Chambers Street which afterwards became Palmo's Opera-House and Burton's Theatre, and then for ten years from 1829 it occupied the apartments of the Clinton Hall Association, on the corner of Nassau and Beekman Streets. Thence, in 1839, it removed to quarters in the building of the Society Library, at the corner of Broadway and Leonard Street. Its next migration carried it to a home of its own at No. 663 Broadway, and yet another removal in 1865 to the building on the corner of Fourth Avenue and Twenty-third Street, which it has lately abandoned for what promises to be a permanent abode at One Hundred and Tenth Street and Amsterdam Avenue. There are few native artists of note who have not been counted among the Academy's members during the last seventy years, and its part in the development of American painting and sculpture has been from the first an honorable and helpful one.

John Stephenson, father of the street railway, began his business career at No. 667 Broadway, and five doors removed, on the same side of the way, is the site of Tripler's Hall, held in pleasant remembrance by every veteran lover of music, for within its newly built walls, in June, 1852, Marietta Alboni made her first appearance in America, to win instant and joyous recognition as perhaps the greatest singer the world has heard since Malibran. She was then less than thirty years old, and in the flush of a splendid womanhood, which lent added charm to her voice, a rich deep contralto, marvellously sweet and uplifting, and of wondrous flexibility and compass. She was not an actress, as her subsequent appearance in opera bore witness, but those who felt her spell will tell you that in her own kingdom she reigned absolute queen, —the greatest contralto of her generation,—and, save Malibran and Lind, no singer of the last century did so much to improve and purify the taste of music-lovers in this country.

Alboni had her full measure of fame yet to win when she crossed the Western ocean, but Henrietta Sontag could point to a long public career, and one almost without a parallel in music, when in September, 1852, she made her first appearance in America at Tripler's Hall. Madame Sontag was at this time well advanced into middle life, but she looked twenty years younger than her age, and had lost little of the personal charm, the grace of soul and body, and the high-bred repose that made her, to quote one of her biographers, "the ideal of a beautiful great lady of the olden time." The years had also dealt most kindly with her voice,—an absolute soprano, pure, penetrating, and of angelic tone, which united flexibility with firmness, and was enhanced besides by an admirable method and an almost perfect execution. If she did not move or touch her hearers, she never failed to charm them, and Americans were quick to recognize the gifts of mind and person which led her to be called the Ninon de l'Enclos of song, and made her, next to Malibran, the best-beloved prima donna of her time. The American visit of the Countess Rossi, as she was known in private life, had a fatal ending, for she died of cholera in Mexico, in June, 1854.

Tripler's Hall became the Metropolitan Theatre in 1854, and a year later the first of Laura Keene's theatres. Then it was Burton's New Theatre, and finally it became the Winter Garden, and the scene of the early triumphs of Edwin Booth. This splendid player, who had served a hard novitiate in California, entered upon his first engagement in New York in May, 1857, but it was not until 1862 that he became the central figure in a series of magnificent revivals of the standard drama at the Winter Garden. These covered a period of five years and included a hundred nights' run of "Hamlet," and a production of "Julius Cæsar," in which the brothers Booth—Junius Brutus, Edwin, and John Wilkes—played Cassius, Brutus, and Marc Antony. Edwin Booth also proved himself supreme as Shylock, Iago, and Richelieu, and as Bertuccio in "The Fool's Revenge." Thereafter, for well-nigh thirty years, he held the stage and was the standard of his time in tragic art. His connection with the Winter Garden, however, ended in March, 1867, when that structure was destroyed by fire, never to be rebuilt for theatrical purposes.

Sixscore years ago the ground now bounded by Waverly Place and Fourth Street and Fourth and Fifth Avenues was a farm owned by Andrew Elliott, "collector and receiver-general of the province of New York," whose roomy house stood on a knoll between the present Ninth and Tenth Streets and just west of Broadway. Elliott returned to England after the Revolution, and his estate became the property of "Baron" Frederick Poelnitz, who sold it in 1790 for the sum of five thousand pounds to Robert Richard Randall. The father of "Captain" Randall, as he was commonly called, was a Scotchman who came to America in 1776, settled in New Orleans, and during the Revolution gained a fortune from privateering ventures against the British. This fortune passed at his death to his bachelor son, who a little later became a resident of New York and the owner of the farm long called after his name. On June 1, 1801, Randall, being "weak in body but of sound disposing mind and memory," made his will in the presence of Alexander Hamilton. When the gift of divers small sums and a few personal belongings had been recorded he paused, in doubt as to how he could most wisely dispose of the remainder of his property.

"How did you accumulate the fortune you possess?" asked Hamilton.

"It was made by my father, and at his death I became his sole heir."

"And how did he acquire it?"

"By honest privateering," was the reply.

And then Hamilton told his client that a fortune thus acquired would be well applied if devoted to the relief of unfortunate and disabled seamen. The will was made in keeping with this suggestion, and though for thirty years vigorous warfare was waged between the heirs and the executors, its validity was finally confirmed by the courts of last resort. It was "Captain" Randall's intention that the Sailors' Snug Harbor thus founded should be built upon his property, and that the twenty-four acres of good farming land which surrounded the mansion house would supply all the grain and vegetables required by the inmates of the institution. The trustees, however, soon discovered that the land could be put to more profitable use. Accordingly, in 1831 they purchased the property on Staten Island where the asylum now stands, while the farm on Broadway was cut up, and, as it could not be sold, rented on ninety-nine-year leases, subject to a renewal for another ninety-nine years. When Randall died his estate yielded an annual income of about four thousand dollars; by 1848 this had increased to nearly forty thousand dollars, by 1870 to upward of one hundred thousand dollars, and at the present time it borders upon four hundred thousand dollars,—all of which is used for the support of aged and disabled seamen,—the growth of the city, with its enhancement of real estate values, having made Sailors' Snug Harbor one of the noblest institutions ever set afoot by a single individual.

The present stroll may well have its ending at Grace Church, erected in 1846 where, at the corner of Tenth Street, the course of Broadway swerving to the west affords all who travel up that thoroughfare full opportunity to see its artistic beauty. Few there are, however, who know that this bend in Broadway was not due to design, but to an obstinate Dutchman's love of a tree. When the last century was young and upper Broadway still a country road, there stood, on the site of the church, a tavern flanked by a greensward and shaded by a tree of unusual size and beauty. Hendrick Brevoort, proprietor of the tavern, long counted this tree among his choicest possessions. Then came the extension of Broadway to Fourteenth Street and the sad discovery by Brevoort that the street as staked out would pass over the ground occupied by the tree under which he smoked his pipe on summer afternoons. Whereupon the tavern-keeper bestirred himself to save it, and putting forth all the influence he possessed, at last succeeded in having the course of Broadway so changed as to make a bend towards the west at Tenth Street, instead of following the straight line originally had in mind by the city surveyors. The extended thoroughfare passed alongside of the tree, but did not demand its sacrifice. Time has since claimed tavern, tree, and Dutchman, but the bend in Broadway remains, and, set off by the Gothic walls of Grace Church, affords one of the most satisfying street views to be had upon Manhattan Island.

VII

Bowery Lane

THE Bowery of modern days is counted by observant travellers the most interesting thoroughfare in America, and not less interesting is the part it played in the past, for it got its name and being from the first settlers of Manhattan. The word bouwerij is Dutch for farm, or country-seat, and the Bowery borrows its name from the fact that it ran through the bowery of Peter Stuyvesant. It had been an Indian trail before it became a country lane, and it remained through long years the only road leading from the upper reaches of the island to the hamlet clustered about Fort Amsterdam. Later still it was the beginning of the post-road to Boston, whereof the mile-stone yet standing in the Bowery, opposite Rivington Street, is a mute and lonely relic. The opening of the Revolution found the Bowery largely built upon as far as Grand Street, and thence to its junction with the present Broadway at Fifteenth Street lined with the country-houses of well-to-do citizens.

Then and for many years thereafter it was the fashionable drive and main highway of the town, and it was not until the early decades of the last century that it was overtaken by the changes that have since made it the most heterogeneous, and, by the same token, the most cosmopolitan street to be found in any American city.

The present pilgrimage, however, has to do with the Bowery of the old days, before half a million alien residents had claimed it for their own or the Collect had been forever buried beneath earth, brick, and mortar. Time was when there was no more beautiful spot on Manhattan Island than the Collect, which covered the territory now bounded by Baxter, White, Elm, Duane, and Park Streets, for it was a sparkling lake, fed by large springs of great reputed purity. The Indians, before the coming of the white man, often pitched their wigwams in the groves that flanked its banks; and the piles of oyster-shells which they left on the western shore led the Dutch to call the place Kalch Hoek, or Shell Point, whence the name of Collect, later applied to the lake itself. The Collect was long a famous fishing-ground,—witness a law of 1734 prohibiting the use of a net in its waters and imposing a fine upon any person catching fish "by any other manner than that of angling,"—while in winter it became a skating-park thronged on moonlit nights with a merry army. Here during the British occupation the future William IV. mastered the graceful art and at the same time played havoc with the hearts of the royalist belles of the town. South of the Fresh Water lay a smaller lake, known as the Little Collect, and upon the strip of ground between them during the later colonial period stood the City Magazine, or Powder-House. The road leading to it from Broadway was called Magazine Street, and is now a part of Pearl.

John Fitch in the summer of 1796, eleven years before Fulton launched the "Clermont," sailed a steamboat upon the Collect. The vessel, we are told, was a ship's yawl, with square stern and round bows, fitted with a screw propeller and a twelve-gallon iron pot that served for a boiler. Though the little craft several times circled the pond at the rate of six miles an hour, no practical results issued from this interesting experiment, and it fell to others to complete the work which Fitch strove through weary years to make his own. His boat was left upon the shore of the pond, and the poor of the neighborhood cut up the woodwork and carried it away for fuel. A model of the original, however, is still treasured by the New York Historical Society. Before the end of the decade in which fell Fitch's experiment the growing city had enfolded the Collect, and the filling of the Little Collect about 1805 was speedily followed by the like obliteration of the larger lake. To-day the city prison and many another gloomy pile cover the spot where of old "the fish leaped and the waters laughed beneath the bows of the Indian's canoe." The extinction of the Collect is not to be regretted, but had the made land, instead of being used for building, been set aside as a public park and planted with trees to suck the moisture from the sodden soil, beauty and healthfulness would have been assured to what is now a densely populated area.

A block south from Chatham Square, Mulberry Street leads westward from Park Row to Mulberry Bend Park. There, until the park was established a few years ago, were Mulberry Bend and the Five Points. Men not yet old recall the Five Points as a place where all the evil passions had their playground; but its interest for the student of an earlier time lies in the fact that it was long a place of execution and that there during the "Great Negro Plot" of

1741 many blacks were burned at the stake. Hughson, the white leader of the plot, if it was a plot, was hanged at the corner of Cherry and Catherine Streets, and the records of those dark days tell how his body "was suspended in chains for many days in the hottest part of the summer, a spectacle for the children, who commented curiously upon the changes in his countenance!" Thus did the Five Points enter upon the career of violence and evil-doing which now has happily become a part of the past.

The Collect's eastern outlet in early times was the Old Wreck Brook, which made its way to the East River on the line of the present Roosevelt Street, through a valley known as Wolfert's Marsh. Hard by this stream, near the intersection of the present Park Row and Pearl Street was the Tea Water spring, whose water for generations was counted the best on the island. Time was when the well at the fort was the only other wholesome source of supply, and as late as 1840 scores of carts were regularly employed in distributing the Tea Water in casks throughout the town. The lessee of the pump there erected advertises in 1796 to deliver water, not only for drinking and tea, but for washing and family use, for four shillings per hogshead; and another advertisement of the same period, offering for lease a house on Reade Street, emphasizes the proximity of the Tea Water Pump as one of the special advantages of the premises. No trace of this spring remains, but the pump was found some years ago in a saloon at No. 126 Chatham Street, and rescued from owners who knew nothing of its origin.

Bowery Lane crossed the Old Wreck Brook near the spring, and then climbed the hill, whereon, close to what is now Chatham Square, Wolfert Webber built the tavern which was long the farthest outlying dwelling on the eastern side of the town. Close at hand, on the north side of Pell Street, just west of Bowery Lane, there stood until a few years ago the house where at a later time Charlotte Temple ended her life. The hapless romance which made her the central figure of Mrs. Rowson's "True Tale" had its beginning, if tradition speaks the truth, in a house which stood aforetime in Art Street, now Astor Place, and it was when repulsed by her lover from the Walton house, in Pearl Street, that, ill and despairing, she found refuge in the hovel where she died.

A reminiscent old gentleman but lately gone from among us has often told the writer that he could recall the time when the Boston stage took its noisy departure from No. 17 Bowery, and when, two doors removed, Bull's Head Tavern gave welcome to the wayfarer. This tavern was a "snug place, with two low stories and a roof whose gabled windows blinked down upon the Bowery. Below were a spacious bar-room with a huge fireplace and cosey corners, always filled with great-coated farmers, stage hands, and stable-boys; a waiting-room for women, a dining-room whose ceiling a tall man would bump his head against, and a kitchen larger than all these rooms put together, where favored patrons toasted their shins and ogled the buxom serving maids. Behind this, and entered from an arched drive-way, was a large court, paved with cobble-stones, from which at the two sides and the rear extended cavernous stables, always a bustling, busy place, from the coming and going at all times of day and night." The Bull's Head was a boyhood haunt of Washington Irving; and one of his biographers tells us that his first promptings to the "rambling propensity" which he confesses was strengthened with his years was got from the coming and going of the rugged folk he saw there,—the Bowery was then the year-round open market for the farmers from a hundred miles to the north and east,—and his enjoyment of the gay and lively scenes at the arrival and departure of the stages, which with bustle and clatter enlivened the little villages between New York and Danbury town.

The Bull's Head remained for half a century the meeting-place of the butchers of the town and the drovers of the country-side. Then it was torn down, and in 1826 a theatre—the New York, soon to be called the American, and not long thereafter to become the Bowery—was erected on its site. The new playhouse, four times burned in after days and as often rebuilt, opened with a company which included Ann Duff and George Barrett, and for fifty years almost every English-speaking actor of note trod its stage. Charlotte Cushman made there her first New York appearance as Lady Macbeth, and John Gilbert his metropolitan début as Sir Edward Mortimer in "The Iron Chest." Thomas Hamblin, long its manager and a tragedian of the robust school; John R. Scott and Edwin Eddy, both of whom followed Forrest at a distance; George Jones, known in old age as the eccentric Count Johannes, but then a young and handsome actor; Priscilla Cooper, later to play her part as lady of the White House during the

Presidency of her husband's father, John Tyler; Danton Marble, one of the first to portray the Yankee upon the stage; James K. Hackett, counted the best Falstaff of his time; Mrs. Shaw, who abandoned her husband to become the wife of Hamblin; Josephine Clifton, the first American actress to play in London; and George Holland, who made his début in seven different parts in one evening,—all these, and many more, had a share in the early glories of the Bowery and helped to give it an abiding hold on the affections of its patrons.

Forrest and the elder Booth were often seen at this theatre, and were the actors best beloved by that singular and now extinct product of New York life, the Bowery boy. The volunteer fire department gave birth to the Bowery boy, who worked for his living on week-days, and on evenings and holidays aimed only to be a dandy and a fireman. "His hair," Dayton tells us, "was one of his chief cares, and from appearance the engrossing object of his solicitude. It was cropped at the back of the head as closely as scissors could cut, while the long front locks were stiffened with bear's grease, and then rolled and brushed until they shone like glass bottles. His face was closely shaven, as beards in any shape

THE OLD BOWERY THEATRE IN 1860

were considered effeminate, and so forbidden by his creed. A black, straight, broad-brimmed hat, polished as highly as a hot iron could effect, was worn with a pitch forward, and a slight inclination to one side, intended to impart a rakish air. A large shirt-collar turned down and loosely fashioned, so as to expose the full proportions of a brawny neck; a black frock-coat with skirts extending below the knee; a flashy satin or velvet vest, cut so low as to expose the entire bosom of a shirt often embroidered; trousers tight to the knee, and thence gradually swelling in size to the bottom, so as nearly to conceal feet encased in well-polished boots,"—these, with much jewelry, much loud perfume, a voice modelled after that of the fire-trumpet, and a language all his own, completed the picture of the Bowery boy,—first at fires, devoted patron of the theatre, and worshipper of good women. He walked with arms akimbo when on parade, and if anybody jostled him he was insulted; and when he was insulted he fought. Rough rather than tough, another of his admiring biographers records that, desirous of punching somebody at all times, he especially liked to punch persons who were rude or cruel to the female sex, and that he scorned to use any weapons save those that nature gave him. King of his little world, few there were in the days of his glory who could compel his reverence. Thackeray, it is said, was once passing through the Bowery; desiring to go to Houston Street, but not certain as to whether he was right in pursuing the direction he had taken, he stepped up to a Bowery boy and asked, "Sir, can I go to Houston Street this way?"

"Yes, I guess yer kin, sonny," was the condescending answer,—"if yer behave yerself."

The Bowery boy went out with the Civil War, and with him went the "palmy days" of the playhouse that had been his chosen haunt. Thereafter the dramas that found a place on its stage were of the noisiest sort, and property-man strove with player for the plaudits of pit and gallery. Finally, in September, 1879, it was opened as the Thalia Theatre, and for a dozen years furnished employment to Marie Geistinger, Sophia Gallmeyer, Kathi Schratt, Ludwig Barnay, Ernst Possart, Adolph Sonnenthal, and other German players of distinction. The Bowery's history as a German theatre ended in 1891. When it was again used it was by Yiddish players, who still appear there, and will doubtless continue to do so until the site is divided into building-lots and the now dingy pile goes the way of its vanished comrades. Mention should be made in passing of the New Bowery, a daring theft of the older theatre's name, which following 1859 stood on the west side of the way, between Canal and Hester Streets. The New Bowery was burned in December, 1866, and the site was never again used for theatrical purposes.

When the Bowery was still a country lane it was flanked in its middle reaches by the farms of the De Lanceys and the Bayards. The De Lancey estate lay between Division and Stanton Streets, and extended to the East River, the homestead standing at what is now the corner of Delancey and Chrystie Streets, while that of the Bayards stretched from Bayard to Prince Streets, and irregularly westward to Macdougal Street. The Bayard homestead crowned the summit of a hill which reached its highest point at what is now the corner of Grand and Mulberry Streets. This eminence, long known as Pleasant Mount, and later still as Bunker Hill, commanded a view of the whole island, and was one of the first places fortified at the outbreak of the Revolution. Tradition has it that it was also a favorite meeting-place for duellists, and the scene of more than one fatal encounter. Bunker Hill's last days, however, were peaceful ones, and for some years before its levelling began, in 1802, it was a summer-garden and pleasuring-place much frequented by the youth of the town.

An old-fashioned, Dutch-roofed structure yet standing at the corner of Prince and Marion Streets, not far from the Bowery, was the last home of James Monroe. The ex-President, after the death of his wife, in 1830, removed to New York and lived with his son-in-law, Samuel L. Gouverneur, once postmaster of the city, at No. 63 Prince Street. He was in feeble health when he came, and on July 4, 1831, he died. His funeral was the most imposing seen in New York up to that time. The body was placed in a vault in the Marble Cemetery, but rests there no longer. The State of Virginia in 1858 asked for its keeping, and the ceremony of removal was accomplished with even more pomp than the original interment. New York, Brooklyn, and Jersey City hung their flags at half-mast and draped their public buildings in black. The coffin lay in state in the Church of the Annunciation in West Fourteenth Street on Friday, July 2, after which it was escorted in long procession to the City Hall. Resting under the flag for a single night, on the morning of July 3 the Seventh Regiment, with colors shrouded, escorted the body on board the steamship " Jamestown" and accompanied it to Richmond, where it was reinterred in Hollywood Cemetery. The Prince Street house shows signs of age and neglect. It stands amid squalid surroundings, and now does duty as a restaurant.

The little city of the dead in which Monroe was first laid to rest fronts Second Street between First and Second Avenues, and is full of legends of the past; but few who visit it know that only a few rods away is a yet more interesting God's Acre. This second and smaller meeting-place of the silent lies in the heart of the block bounded by the Bowery and Second Avenue and Second and Third Streets. Rows of tenements on every side hide it from view, and only an iron gate-way set in between two houses in Second Street gives hint of its existence. One who gains entrance to this gate-way, however, finds at the farther end of a narrow alley a tiny burial-yard, thickly strewn with graves, marked not by tombstones, but by slabs of marble set in the enclosing wall. Many of these record the names of men closely associated with the growth and progress of the town, and recall the time when the nook in which their owners were laid to rest stood amid spreading fields and country lanes,—"a place of interment for gentlemen." Years ago the northward march of the town engulfed the walled-up cemetery, but did not sweep it away, and the old-time silence that has once more claimed it for its own prompts the hope that no further change may come to this bit of hallowed earth.

Crossing again to the westward side of the Bowery, one finds St. Patrick's standing sombre and venerable at the corner of Prince and Mott Streets, fenced in by its graveyard. The region round about, sparsely settled when the building of this church was begun in 1815, is now one of the most thickly populated districts in the town, but the change has little meaning for those who take their rest within the shadow of its walls. Here is the grave of the Venetian poet, Lorenzo Daponte, who died in near-by Spring Street at the age of ninety, and was followed to his burial by such mourners as Woodworth and Halleck; while not far away a plain white slab tells the passer-by that Pierre de Landais sleeps beneath it. An officer in the French navy, Landais entered the service of the United States at the outbreak of the Revolution, and soon rose to the command of a frigate and the title of admiral, but in the fight between the "Serapis" and the "Bonhomme Richard," Landais, who fought by the rules laid down in his text-books, incurred the name of coward, while Paul Jones, by his impetuous and undisciplined bravery, won that of hero. Cited before the naval committee of Congress, its members refused to accept Landais's explanations, and he was thrown out of the service. He became a resident of New York after this disgrace, and again and again made futile appeals to Congress for restitution to his rank and arrears of pay. A dividend of prize-money, earned at the beginning of the Revolution and paid in 1790, gave him a small annuity, and on this scanty income he managed to maintain the habits and exterior of a gentleman. He wore the Revolutionary cockade to the last, and on great occasions regularly donned his old Continental uniform. Thus for forty years Landais walked the streets in proud and solitary poverty, until at the age of eighty-seven, as his epitaph says, he "disappeared" from life.

A little less than two hundred years ago there flourished at the corner of the present Warren and Greenwich Streets a popular place of amusement called Vauxhall. This name was transferred in 1798 to a resort established by one Delacroix at the old Bayard homestead on Bunker Hill; and thence was shifted, a few years later, to a pleasure-garden at the upper end of the Bowery. This last Vauxhall Garden, which replaced a real garden wherein for half a century Jacob Sperry, a Swiss, grew flowers and fruit, extended from the Bowery to Broadway, and from Fourth Street to Astor Place, being surrounded by a high board fence. A theatre, in which occasional performances were held, "garden walks shaded by trees and ornamented by beds of shrubs and flowers, and small boxes fitted up to represent mystic bowers" were features of the Bowery Vauxhall, which ran its prosperous course for a long term of years. Later, as the city grew towards it, it became a favorite place for public meetings and the stamping-ground of the campaign orator. Lot by lot, however, it was gradually shorn of its goodly proportions. In 1827 the opening of Lafayette Place cut it in two, and, though successive managers sought to revive its dwindling patronage by the aid of cheap concerts, negro minstrelsy, and calico balls, in 1855 its existence came to an end. Now the Astor Library stands quite in the centre of the vanished garden.

Clinton Hall, less than a block away, occupies the former site of the Astor Place Opera-House, which, when opened to the public, was counted the best-appointed theatre in America. Its builders designed to make it the home of Italian opera, and its opening in November, 1847, was the great social event of the day. "Ernani" was the first opera produced on its stage, and the cast included Teresa Truffi as Elvira. Over few singers of other days do veteran opera-goers wax so eloquent as they do over Truffi the magnificent. Good judges agree that she was not a great singer in the strict sense of the word, but they will tell you that her voice and style were sympathetic and full of charm. Nature, moreover, had created her when in one of its generous moods, and she trod the boards unconscious of her beauty, yet a very queen among women. She was greatest in tragic *rôles*. America has not seen her equal as Lucrezia, and she was wholly admirable in Elvira, in Donna Anna, and in the impassioned Jewess of Verdi's "Narbucco." Opera's single season in Astor Place, however, had financial failure written at its close, and when the new theatre in the spring of 1849 came again into notice it was as the scene of a riot, an outcome of the enmity existing between Edwin Forrest and Macready, the English tragedian, in which more than two hundred people were killed or wounded. Three years later the opera-house became the New York Theatre, and in 1854 the Mercantile Library Association built it over into Clinton Hall.

Cooper Union, which at Eighth Street splits the Bowery in twain, sending one half up town to be Third Avenue, and the other to be Fourth Avenue, stands as a monument to an uncommon man. Peter Cooper as a boy—he was born in 1791—worked in his father's hat-shop, then in a brewery, and finally when he was seventeen he became an apprentice to a coach-maker. His chance came to him in 1812, when the second war with England closed our ports to foreign manufactures and caused a demand for native textiles. Cooper invented a machine for shearing rough cloth, and made money from it before the close of the war. Then with the capital he had acquired he turned his factory into a cabinet-shop, later taking up the manufacture of glue and isinglass. His glue-factory is still in operation, and with it he secured the nucleus of what afterwards became a great fortune, part of which he devoted in his old age to founding an institution for "the instruction and improvement of the inhabitants of the United States in practical science and art." The history of Cooper Institute, enlarged by gifts and bequests from his family, has proved the generous wisdom of its founder. Its utmost capacity has been taxed from the first, and thousands have gone forth from its portals fitted to discharge with skill and capacity the tasks set for them in the world's workshops.

Our stroll has brought us now to the borders of the buried farm which gave the Bowery its name. The estate which Peter Stuyvesant bought for himself in 1647, paying therefor six thousand four hundred guilders, was bounded by Sixth and Seventeenth Streets and by Fourth Avenue and the East River. The house he built upon it and in which he ended his days stood, until destroyed by fire in 1778, a little east of Third Avenue and just north of Tenth Street, near the site of St. Mark's Church, in which he takes his rest. The houses of the workers on the farm were grouped close together, as a protection against marauding Indians; in their wake followed a tavern and a blacksmith-shop, and Stuyvesant erected a chapel at his own expense, in which Hermanus Van Hoboken, school-master of New Amsterdam, read service every Sunday. Such was the origin of

Bowery Village, which preserved its existence for the better part of two hundred years. The townsfolk made it a turning-place in their pleasure-jaunts, or in time of scourge sought refuge there, and there in Leisler's time the commissioners from New England, declining to enter the town because of small-pox, met with those of New York to discuss the invasion of Canada.

Threescore years ago Bowery Village was swallowed up by the ever-growing city, and of it only one visible sign now remains,—the diagonal course of Stuyvesant Street, one of the oldest of the village lanes, which, escaping the fate of its fellows, still bids defiance to the lines of the City Plan. Time and change have also claimed both of the houses erected by Stuyvesant's descendants on the lands which he left to them. One of these, called Petersfield, stood by the East River shore, near the present Avenue A and Sixteenth Street, and was reached by a winding lane that led from the pear-tree of pleasant memory at Third Avenue and Thirteenth Street. The other, built by Nicholas William Stuyvesant, stood between First and Second Avenues and Eighth and Ninth Streets, with entrance from the Bowery near Sixth Street.

Tompkins and Stuyvesant Squares are both

within the limits of the Stuyvesant farm, the former being part of a whilom salt-marsh of many acres, bordered in the old days by low sand-hills, and known as the Stuyvesant Meadows. This marsh stretched from Avenue A to the East River and from Houston to Twelfth Streets. Seventy years ago underground drainage and surface-filling made its sodden reaches available for building purposes, and on its western border arose Tompkins Square. Stuyvesant Square, five city blocks to the northward, is one of the out-of-the-way corners of Manhattan which most vividly suggest the folk and customs of a by-gone time. What with its old Quaker meeting-house, and beside it, forever unfinished, St. George's Church, the aspect of Stuyvesant Square is much the same as when in the middle years of the last century it was a centre of fashionable life, save that the houses which flank it are now used for lodging or business purposes, and no longer dispense the stately hospitality of an earlier day.

William M. Evarts lived for many years and died at No. 231 Second Avenue, a brownstone mansion hard by Stuyvesant Square. A house at No. 118 East Tenth Street was long the home of Richard Grant White; and just across the way lived John H. Johnson, with whom Walt Whitman found a welcome whenever during his later years he left his home in Camden to spend a few days in "mast-hemmed Manhattan." The house formerly numbered 181 East Thirteenth Street once had Bayard Taylor and Richard Henry Stoddard for joint tenants, while a more modern structure covers the site of the dwelling at No. 124 East Twenty-sixth Street in which Herman Melville ended his days. Melville was a born romancer, and the tales he wrote of his wanderings and experiences in the South Sea gave him an audience as far-reaching as the English-speaking race. Then he fell into a neglect none who has read his books can explain; and so long did he survive his early fame that when he died in 1891 the men and women of a new generation learned for the first time that such a man as Herman Melville had once lived and won and held the favor of his fellows.

VIII

Lispenard's Meadows

TIME was, and that within the memory of men still living, when Lispenard's Meadows were a conspicuous and familiar feature of the olden town. One of the subdivisions of the estate known successively as the Duke's Farm, the King's Farm, the Queen's Farm, and finally, when it became the property of the Corporation of Trinity, as the Church Farm, was the Domine's Hook, lying between the Hudson, a swamp where is now West Broadway, the present Reade Street, and the southern edge of the valley through which ran the western outlet of the Collect or Fresh Water Pond.

This outlet took its course to the Hudson on the line of Canal Street and to the north and south of it lay some seventy acres of swamp, which Anthony Rutgers in 1730 offered to drain on condition that the reclaimed land be given to him. " The said swamp," ran his petition to the king and Council, "is constantly filled with standing water, for which there is no natural vent, and being covered with bushes and small trees is by the stagnation and rotteness of it become exceedingly dangerous and of fatal consequence to all the inhabitants of the north part of the city bordering on the same, they being subject to very many diseases and distempers, which by all physicians and by long experience are imputed to the unwholesome vapors arising thereby; and as the said swamp is upon a level with the waters of the Hudson and the South (East) Rivers, no person has ever yet attempted to clear the same, nor ever can under a grant thereof which is to expire with the next new governor; for the expense of clearing the same will be so great, and the length of time in doing the same such that it will never be attempted, but by a grantee of the fee simple thereof; and as the same can be of no benefit until it is cleared, so no person has hitherto accepted a grant of the said land, but the same hath lain and still remains unimproved and uncultivated, to the great prejudice and annoyance of the adjacent farms, particularly to a farm of your petitioner adjoining thereto, which your petitioner, having been to great expense in settling, cannot prevail on any tenant to take the same, or get any servants to continue there for any time, while the said swamp remains in its present state."

The Council granted the request of the enterprising Anthony, and gave him the fee of the swamp on condition that he should pay for it "a moderate quit-rent," and that he should "clear it and drain it within a year." Young Leonard Lispenard, who held the Domine's Hook by lease from Trinity, made love to and married the daughter of his neighbor, and when Rutgers, having first cleared, drained, and converted into good pasture a considerable part of the swamp, reached the end of his days, the meadows passed to this daughter and her husband, and thenceforth were known as Lispenard's Meadows. The lowland lying on each side of the stream from the Collect, however, remained unimproved until the opening years of the last century, when it was straightened, deepened, and planked, making a ten-foot canal in a street one hundred feet in width. This canal was spanned at Broadway by a stone bridge, raised above the surface of the meadows, and approached by a narrow embankment from either side, while another bridge at Church Street was used as a short cut by the inhabitants of Greenwich in going to and from the city. It was not long, however, before the growing town reached and passed Canal Street, and little by little the whole marshy area of Lispenard's Meadows was drained, filled, and covered with city blocks. Now a sewer far below the surface of Canal Street carries to the Hudson the flow of water from the ancient springs that once fed the buried Collect, while, save for an occasional wet cellar, there remains no trace of the swamp that once made the whole valley a dangerous quagmire.

About the time that Anthony Rutgers began to drain the vanished meadows he built a fine dwelling near the present corner of Thomas Street and Broadway. "He surrounded his habitation," Valentine tells us, "with elegant shrubbery in the geometrical style of rural gardening of those days. Long walks, bordered with boxwood and shaded and perfumed with flowering shrubs, extended in various directions in the parterre bordering the house; the favorite orchard extended along the southerly side of the mansion, while the pasture-lands and cultivated fields extended towards the north." It was "a charming rural residence," writes Valentine; and he adds that "even in after years, when its quiet and domestic characteristics had given place to the festive incidents attached to a public resort, the advertisement of the proprietor expressed it as judged to be the most rural and pleasing retreat in the city."

Rutgers died about 1750, and his home passed by lease to one John Jones, who transformed it into a summer-garden and gave it the name of Ranelagh. Jones's advertisements in the *Weekly Post Boy* describe Ranelagh as "a popular resort of very elegant excellence," equipped with "all conveniences for breakfasting and every entertainment for ladies and gentlemen," with "a complete band in attendance every Monday and Thursday during the summer in a large dancing-hall," surrounded by "ornamental gardens laid out in the geometrical style." Ranelagh had from the first a prosperous career, and for a score of years, in the language of the not over-modest Jones, held the lead "among those suburban places of amusement where music, dancing, and feasting constitute their share in the amusements of the hour." It was demolished in 1773 to furnish a site for the New York Hospital, but it left a worthy successor in Brannan's Garden, established about the year 1765 on the north side of the Meadows, near the present crossing of Spring and Hudson Streets.

Brannan's Garden fronted the Greenwich

Road, and a cue to the trade which brought golden guineas to its proprietor is found in the narrative of the Rev. William Burnaby, an English traveller who visited the city in the last days of the colonial period. "The amusements," writes his reverence, "are balls and sleighing-parties in the winter, and in the summer going in parties upon the water and fishing, or making excursions into the country. There are several houses pleasantly situated up the East River, near New York, where it is common to have turtle-feasts. These happen once or twice a week. Thirty or forty gentlemen and ladies meet and dine together; drink tea in the afternoon, fish and amuse themselves until evening, and then return home in Italian chaises, a gentleman and lady in each chaise." Such a party, homeward bound from Turtle Bay, would be pretty certain to lay its route by way of the Greenwich Road and to halt at Brannan's for a final sup before entering the town. "And a brave sight it must have been," to quote Janvier, "when the long line of carriages got under way again and went dashing along the causeway over Lispenard's green meadows, while the silvered harness of the horses and the brilliant varnish of the chaises gleamed and sparkled in the rays of nearly level sunshine from the sun that was setting there a hundred years and more ago."

When Brannan's modest but comfortable road-house still gave welcome to turtle-feasters and other folk out for a holiday there lay to the north of Lispenard's Meadows, between Charlton and West Houston Streets, a swampy tract, through which Minetta Water took its way to the Hudson. This stream was formed by the union of two rivulets, which met in the middle of the block bounded by Fifth and Sixth Avenues and Eleventh and Twelfth Streets. Thence the creek flowed in a southerly direction to Fifth Avenue, below Clinton Place; then curving to the west it threaded the marsh that later was transformed into Washington Square, and ran parallel with and a little south of Minetta and Downing Streets, across West Houston, to the swamp already mentioned. Near the outlet of the stream, and between it and Lispenard's Meadows, rose Richmond Hill, the southwestern outjut of the chain of sand-mounds called the Zandtberg, which stretched in a long curve from the present Lafayette Place to about the intersection of Hudson and Vandam Streets. The creek expanded into a lake at the foot of the hill, and " from the crest of this small eminence was an enticing prospect,—on the south the woods and dells and winding road from the lands of Lispenard, through the valley where was Borrowson's Tavern; and on the north and west the plains of Greenwich Village made up a rich prospect to gaze on."

The charms of this "prospect" caused Abraham Mortier, commissary to his Majesty's forces, to purchase Richmond Hill in 1760 and build there a wooden house of "massive architecture, with a lofty portico supported by Ionic columns, the front walls decorated with pilasters of the same order, and its whole appearance distinguished by a palladian character of rich though sober ornament." A fine house it must have been, judged by the standards of the period, and Mortier made it the centre of a liberal hospitality, counting among his guests Sir Jeffrey, afterwards Lord Amherst, who had his headquarters there when he had ended the campaigns which broke the power of France in America. Washington occupied the house in 1776, and after the retreat of the patriot army it was tenanted by various British officers of high rank, including Howe and Cornwallis.

John Adams when he took office as Vice-President chose Richmond Hill for his residence, and

Mrs. Adams in her letters pays tribute to the loveliness of their home. "The venerable oaks and broken ground, covered with wild shrubs, which surround me," she wrote in 1790, "give a natural beauty to the spot which is truly enchanting. A lovely variety of birds serenade me morning and evening, rejoicing in their liberty and security, for I have, as much as possible, prohibited the grounds from invasion, and sometimes almost wished for game-laws, when my orders have not been regarded. The partridge, the woodcock, and the pigeon are too great temptations for the sportsman to withstand."

Gulian C. Verplanck, writing in "The Talisman" for 1829, gives us a glimpse of the interior of Richmond Hill at this period in his description of a Vice-Presidential dinner-party. "There in the centre of the table," he writes, quoting one of the guests, "sat Vice-President Adams in full dress, with his bag and solitaire, his hair frizzed out each side of his face, as you see it in Stuart's older pictures of him. On his right sat Baron Steuben. On his left was Mr. Jefferson, who had just returned from France, conspicuous in red waistcoat and breeches, the fashion of Versailles. Opposite sat Mrs. Adams, with her cheerful, intelligent face. She was placed between the courtly Count de Moustier, the French embassador, in his red-heeled shoes and ear-rings, and the grave, polite, and formally bowing Mr. Van Birket, the learned and able envoy of Holland. There, too, was Chancellor Livingston, then still in the prime of life, so deaf as to make conversation with him difficult, yet so overflowing with wit, eloquence, and information that while listening to him the difficulty was forgotten. The rest of them were members of Congress and of our legislature, some of them no inconsiderable men. Being able to talk French, a rare accomplishment in America at that time, a place was assigned to me next the count. The dinner was served up after the fashion of that day, abundant and, as was then thought, splendid. De Moustier, after taking a little soup, kept an empty plate before him, and declined all the luxuries of the table that were pressed upon him, from the roast-beef down to the lobsters. We were all in perplexity to know how he could dine, when at length his own body-cook, a warm pie of truffles and game in his hand, came bustling through the crowd of waiters, and placed it before the count, who, reserving a share to himself, distributed the rest among his neighbors, of whom being one, I can attest to the truth of the story and the excellence of the pâté."

The last considerable occupant of Richmond Hill, again to quote Verplanck, " was Counsellor Benson, afterwards governor of the Danish Islands, a man who had travelled in every part of the world, knew everything, and talked all languages. I recollect dining here in company with thirteen gentlemen, none of whom I ever saw before, but all pleasant fellows, all men of education and some note,—the counsellor a Norwegian, I the only American, the rest of every different nation in Europe, and no two of the same, and all of us talking bad French together."

Before Benson's tenancy and this cosmopolitan dinner-party Richmond Hill had been the home of Aaron Burr, who, in May, 1797, leased the premises for sixty-nine years. He lived there before and during his term as Vice-President, and there his daughter, the lovely and ill-fated Theodosia, dispensed a charming hospitality to guests who included the most eminent men and women of the period. Louis Philippe, Talleyrand, Volney, and Brant, the Indian chieftain, were among those who had welcome at Richmond Hill when Burr was its master and his star still in the ascendant. Then came the duel with

Hamilton on that July morning in 1804, and presently the survivor of that fatal encounter left his stately home never to return to it.

One incident of Burr's occupancy of Richmond Hill throws a pleasant sidelight on his romantic career. Journeying on a summer's day from Albany to New York, and stopping at a tavern in Kingston, he was shown some drawings which gave evidence of exceptional talent and which he was told were the work of a wagon-maker's apprentice named John Vanderlyn. Burr sent for the youth, learned his condition, and dismissed him with the remark. "When you wish to change your situation, put a clean shirt in your pocket, come to New York, and ask for Colonel Burr." A few months afterwards, while Burr was at breakfast, a country-boy knocked at the door and asked to see him. The servant refused admission to the visitor, but forcing his way into the breakfast-room, he walked straight to the table, pulled a coarse, clean shirt from his pocket, and silently laid it before Burr.

The action at once recalled to Burr the interview in the tavern at Kingston, and, taken perhaps in some measure by its oddity, he adopted Vanderlyn as a *protégé,* and ere long sent him to Paris. There the young man justified the good opinion of his patron, and in a few years took rank among the most accomplished painters of his time, winning greater honor on the continent of Europe than had been accorded to any American artist. His fortunes were at the flood when, in 1808, his whilom patron arrived in Europe, self-exiled on account of the encounter with Hamilton. Vanderlyn, to his credit be it said, remained faithful to Burr when all the rest of the world seemed to have abandoned the fallen man. When Burr was in humble lodgings in London "at eight shillings a week," and when, we are told by his biographer, "one American friend only was admitted to the secret," Vanderlyn was undoubtedly the "one." Finally, it was through Vanderlyn that Burr, in 1812, was enabled to return to America, the former parting with some of his canvases to furnish his friend with passage-money. Vanderlyn, however, was always chary of speaking of Burr's experience abroad, especially when the information was wanted for the press. Soon after Burr's death an author in New York set out to write his biography, and called on Vanderlyn for material without success. "But tell me something about Burr's private life," said the writer. "You had better let Burr's private life alone," was the artist's significant reply, and there the interview ended.

Vanderlyn's later career, like that of Burr, was a clouded and bitter one. He survived his early triumphs and his friends, and towards the end younger and more tactful men elbowed him rudely in an overcrowded field. New York was the home of his glooming age, but he went often to Kingston, allured no doubt by the grateful associations that clung to the place of his birth. One morning in September, 1852, he landed from a Hudson River steamboat in a feeble condition, and set out to walk to Kingston, two and a half miles distant. Fatigue soon overcame him, and from a friend who found him sitting by the roadside he begged a shilling for the transportation of his baggage, adding that he was sick and penniless. He secured a small back room at one of the village inns, and his friend went quietly about among a few of his acquaintances with a subscription-list for his maintenance. Funds for the purpose were promptly pledged, but they were never needed. A few mornings after his arrival Vanderlyn was found lifeless in bed. Death, merciful in its summons, had come to him while he slept.

The last days of Richmond Hill, where Vanderlyn was often a guest, were those of an humbled aristocrat compelled to dwell amid unwonted surroundings. When the hill, with the rest of the Zandtberg range, was levelled,—to the end that the lowlands thereabouts might be filled in,—the house was gradually lowered to the present street grade and moved back to the line of Charlton Street and a little east of Varick. It became the Richmond Hill Theatre in 1831, and in the following year the temporary home of an Italian opera company. One of the members of this organization was Adelaide Pedrotti, an artist then almost unknown, but whose sympathetic mezzo-soprano voice, queenly presence, and impassioned acting won her a host of admirers. The primo-basso of the company was Luciano Fornasari, whose noble voice and Jove-like bearing—the maids and matrons of the period voted him one of the handsomest men they had ever seen—won him a welcome not less cordial than that accorded to Pedrotti. Mismanagement coupled with lack of financial support, however, brought opera's single season at Richmond Hill to a disastrous end. After that the old house, falling on still more evil times, passed through the gradations of circus, menagerie, and tavern, and in 1849 was demolished to make way for the row of brick houses that can still be seen in Charlton Street.

The region of Lispenard's Meadows holds the sites of two other vanished playhouses. A familiar figure in the New York of seventy years ago was Lorenzo Daponte, an Italian poetaster, whose satirical verse had caused his exile from Venice, and who later became a teacher of languages in America. Daponte had taken a lively interest in the attempt to make Richmond Hill a home of song, and when it failed resolved to establish an Italian opera in New York by subscription. His efforts proved successful, and in November, 1833, the Italian Opera House, located at the southwest corner of Leonard and Church Streets, was opened to the public by a company which bore the name of its manager, the Cavaliere di Rivafinoli. Daponte's venture, however, was born under an evil star. None of the members of the Rivafinoli troupe was a singer of high quality, and the close of the first season witnessed also the closing of the Italian Opera-House as a home of opera. It became the National Theatre in 1836, and for a time had the elder Wallack for its manager, but was burned in 1846, and its site is now occupied by a row of business buildings.

The playhouse built in 1826 by General Charles W. Sanford on what was Laurens Street near Canal shared a like fate. Sanford named his theatre in honor of Lafayette, and it was the largest and finest in the America of its day. Fire, however, claimed it in April, 1829, and St. Alphonsus's Church stands now on its site.

Great are the changes that have swept over Lispenard's Meadows during the last hundred years. When in 1807 the vestry of Trinity Church began the erection of St. John's Chapel on Varick Street between Beach and Laight, wiseacres railed at the folly of building so fine a structure in so remote and forbidding a quarter, for cattle were still pastured on the meadows to the west, and the outlook from the new church's marshy site was over an unshaded waste of rushes and brambles. St. John's, however, was not long without worshippers. Hudson Square, or St. John's Park, covering the block bounded by Varick, Beach, Hudson, and Laight Streets, was laid out as a private pleasure-ground, and when it had been graded, planted, and fenced in, wide-fronted, red-brick houses arose around it, the homes of men of wealth and distinction. Most of the names of these householders, Mines tells us, "had been known in the colonial days,

The families of Alexander Hamilton, General Schuyler, and General Morton were among them, as were also the Aymars, Drakes, Lydigs, Coits, Lords, Delafields, and Hunters. Each resident of the square had his own key to the gates of the park, to which all outsiders were denied admission; and the neighborhood formed an exclusive coterie, into which parvenu wealth could find no passport."

St. John's Park remained for many years an abiding-place of polite society, but fashion moved away in the early fifties. Then little by little the region fell from its high estate, and in the year 1869 the park was buried from sight by the four-acre freight-depot of the Hudson River Railroad Company. The houses that surrounded the park are still there, but all are tenements, with lines of wash-tubs stretched along hall-ways through which one might drive a coach-and-four; stovepipes run into fireplaces in which one might set a dining-table, and cot-beds planted thick in parlors that look like ball-rooms turned into rag-shops. One of these old houses, No. 36 Beach Street, now packed with a Sicilian contingent, was the home for many years of John Ericsson, the inventor. There he did the work which made him one of the famous men of the world, and there he died in 1889, when far past the age of eighty.

Ericsson's life in Beach Street was that of a recluse. He gave himself no recreation, save changing from one form of occupation to another; and one of the reasons he was wont to offer for not joining in the exodus from St. John's Park was the ungallant one that the ladies had ceased to call upon him there. Life was too short for the tasks he had taken in hand, and he guarded himself against those who had no specific business with him as a miser guards his gold. Yet the impulses of a kindly and generous nature remained strong within him to the last, and his biographer tells us that "the walls that enclosed him were never so impenetrable that the cry of distress could not reach him. It was the rule of his house that no one who applied for food should be turned away empty; he was always ready to fill from his own the coal-bins of the distressed widows of the neighborhood, and he had a pension-roll as long as that of a grand-duke. His affection for his native land never ceased; rather, it increased as he advanced in years, and he was constantly making gifts to Sweden and to Swedes. Once the case of a fellow-countryman who was in distress came to his ears, and he instantly helped the man out of trouble. Afterwards he found that the man's birthday fell on the same date as his own. He made no note of the man's name or address, but every year drew a check for one hundred dollars which he sent on his birthday to the poor stranger, and the stubs of these checks were found among his papers after his death." Need one doubt that the reputation Ericsson enjoyed in his neighborhood was that of the ever-ready friend of the poor and friendless, or that he had no sincerer mourners than the humble folk among whom he ended his days?

Though time has taken all of the brave men and gracious women who once lived under the shadow of its spire, old St. John's itself still faces on Varick Street, sombre and unaltered, a stately link between the present and the past. Its boy choir, long one of the most notable in America, still furnishes splendid music to the worshippers, while those who visit the church of a Saturday morning can witness the dispensation of New York's most curious charity,—the Leake Dole of Bread. The Dole, in constant operation since 1792, is a bequest by John Leake, who with John Watts founded the Leake and Watts Orphan House, still in existence in this city.

The portion of his will in which the bequest is made reads as follows:

"I hereby give and bequeath unto the rector and inhabitants of the Protestant Episcopal Church of the State of New York one thousand pounds, put out at interest, to be laid out in the annual income in sixpenny wheaten loaves of bread and distributed on every Sabbath morning, after divine service, to such poor as shall appear most deserving."

Leake's wish has been faithfully carried out with one exception: forty-odd years ago the distributing station was removed from Trinity Church to St. John's, and at the same time, to obviate publicity and spare the pride of the recipients, the weekly day of distribution was changed from Sunday to Saturday. Thus every Saturday eighty loaves of fresh bread are delivered into a recess of St. John's, and piled upon a long settee in the vestibule, where those "appearing to be most deserving" either call or send for them. The Dole has eighteen beneficiaries at the present time, and others are constantly waiting to take the places of those claimed by death. The loaves are distributed in varying numbers, regulated by the size of the family, and, though the pensioners are allowed to enter the vestry and help themselves, it is a matter of record that not once has any one made the mistake of taking an extra loaf. Some of these pensioners are not only communicants of Trinity Church, but people who at one time were among the most wealthy of the congregation. Now in impoverished age they gladly accept the helpful if modest charity which serves to keep green the memory of its founder, and the sight of their weekly visit to old St. John's holds first place among the abiding memories which attend upon a stroll through and around Lispenard's Meadows.

IX

Old Greenwich

OLD New York still lingers in Greenwich Village. Few apartment-houses, but brick and wooden cottages, are to be found in nearly all the thoroughfares that lie within its boundaries. Some of these have quaint decorations, others odd little side-yards and small additions, the after-thought of negligent builders, and all give evidence of the cheerful place the village must have been a few score years ago. Here and there an alley widens into a court shaded with trees; while the Virginia-creeper and the wistaria run riot in other rear premises, scaling dead walls and helping by their greenery to attract the eye and the interest of the passing stranger. Here, too, the hum of the city is hushed to a murmur; there is no stir save when the children are let out from school; and loitering in these quiet thoroughfares one sees in imagination the sedate and respectable folk who trod their paves when Greenwich Village was an entity, and not a tradition.

And this is as it should be, for, the vicinity of the Battery excepted, this corner of New York is the oldest habitation of white men on the Island of Manhattan. Red men lived here in an earlier time. When Minetta Water was still a purling trout-stream and Henry Hudson had yet to make acquaintance with the river that bears his name, fertile, wooded fields stretched from its western bank to the Hudson, and among these fields, near the site of the present Gansevoort Market, lay the Indian village of Sappokanican. Peter Minuit, first of the Dutch governors, knew good land when he saw it, and after he had bought the Island of Manhattan from the Indians he set apart the loamy plain of Sappokanican as one of the farms to be reserved for the special use of the Dutch West India Company. Wouter Van Twiller, the second Dutch governor, was also an excellent judge of land, and, having ever a lively regard for his own interests, he appropriated the Bossen Bouwerie, or Farm in the Woods, as it was set down in the deeds, as his own private tobacco-plantation.

Van Twiller's thrifty conversion of public property to private uses occurred soon after he assumed the governorship in the spring of 1633, and the house which he built the same year on the lands of which he had made himself both grantor and grantee was the first dwelling erected on Manhattan Island north of the environs of Fort Amsterdam. This house stood in the edge of the woodland, a little to the northward of where now is the dock of the Cunard steamers, at the foot of Clarkson Street, and though the records fail to make clear whether or not the Bossen Bouwerie reverted to the West India Company after Van Twiller was recalled in disgrace, they give us now and then a glimpse of the hamlet that gradually grew up about it. Stuyvesant makes a passing reference in one of his papers to "the few houses at Sappokanigan," and there is mention of the village by the Labadist missionaries Dankers and Sluyter, who spent some time upon Manhattan while seeking a home for their sect. "We crossed over the island," runs an entry in their journal under date of September 7, 1679, "which takes about three-quarters of an hour to do, and came to the North River, which we followed a little within the woods to Sappokanikee. There we rested ourselves and drank some good beer, which refreshed us. We continued along the shore to the city, where we arrived early in the evening, very much fatigued, having walked this day about forty miles. I must add, in passing through this island we often encountered such a sweet smell in the air that we stood still; for we did not know what it was we were meeting."

Rum and warfare had before this made an end of the Indian village of the first days. Its Dutch successor, however, grew from year to year, and the opening of the eighteenth century found the latter a thriving settlement, connected with the town below by a road which followed in the main the line of Greenwich Street. Then, in or about 1711, the conquering English having small liking for Dutch names, the Bossen Bouwerie became Greenwich Village; and ere long, attracted perhaps by this change, Captain Peter Warren of the royal navy chose it for his home. A fine figure of a man and every inch a hero was this Captain Warren, who died Sir Peter Warren and a vice-admiral of the Red Squadron, and the list of whose honors ended with a tomb in Westminster Abbey and an epitaph penned by Samuel Johnson. The good doctor tells us in this epitaph that Warren "derived his descent from an ancient family of Ireland," and the fighting qualities of his ancestors appear to have served him well, for when he was only twenty-four years old he had already won the command of a ship with which he helped to wrest Gibraltar from Spain.

This was in 1727, and in the following year he was on the American station in the frigate "Solebay." He was here again in 1737, and in 1741 commanded a squadron of sixteen sail in West Indian waters, where in something less than five months he captured twenty-four prizes, one of them with a lading of plate valued at two hundred and fifty thousand pounds. These prizes found their way to New York, and Stephen De Lancey acted for Captain Warren in their condemnation and sale at prices which, according to the columns of the *Weekly Post Boy,* assured handsome profits both to principal and agent. Captain Warren at the same time, with the luck that appears to have attended all his ventures, won a prize more precious than his French and Spanish loot, for during one of his holidays ashore he courted and married pretty Susannah De Lancey, the daughter of his agent. Then it was that he chose Greenwich as his home, purchasing an estate of some three hundred acres near the river, which was later enlarged by a gift of land voted to him by the city for his part in the capture of Louisburg.

The home which Captain Warren built for his

bride stood on rising ground near the present intersection of Charles and Bleecker Streets, and was flanked by a lawn that reached down to the water-side. It was a prodigiously fine house for the period, with the main entrance from the east, and at the rear a broad veranda which commanded the view westward to the Jersey Highlands and southward to the Staten Island hills. Here the Captain dispensed such hospitality as might be expected of a man with whom picking up a Spanish plate-ship or French merchantman was a commonplace occurrence, and here in the fulness of time his wife bore him three daughters. His residence in Greenwich, however, came soon to an end, and after 1747, when he was elected a member of Parliament for the city of Westminster, America saw no more of him. His wife, who long survived him, also ended her days in England, and there their daughters grew to womanhood and found titled husbands. Charlotte, the eldest, became Countess of Abingdon; Ann, the second daughter, married Charles Fitzroy, afterwards Baron Southampton; and Susannah, the youngest, became the wife of Colonel William Skinner. Susannah's romance ended in the early death of herself and her husband, but she left a daughter to inherit her third of Sir Peter's lands and moneys.

When Lady Warren died the Greenwich estate was partitioned in a somewhat novel way, the story being thus recounted in all deeds for the property: "In pursuance of the powers given in the said antenuptial deeds the trustees therein named, on March 31, 1787, agreed upon a partition of the said lands, which agreement was with the approbation and consent of the cestui que trusts, to wit: Earl and Lady Abingdon, and Charles Fitzroy and Ann his wife, the said Susannah Skinner the second not then having arrived at age. In making the partition, the premises were divided into three parts on a survey made thereof and marked A, B, and C; and it was agreed that such partition should be made by each of the trustees naming a person to throw dice for and in behalf of their respective cestui que trusts, and that the person who should throw the highest number should have parcel A; the one who should throw the next highest number, parcel B; and the one who should throw the lowest number, parcel C,—for the persons whom they respectively represented; and the premises were partitioned accordingly."

The homestead, with fifty-five acres of land,

fell by the turn of the dice to Lady Abingdon, and a little later passed into the possession of Abijah Hammond, who, in 1819, sold the mansion house, with the square bounded by Tenth, Bleecker, Charles, and Perry Streets, to Abraham Van Nest. This property remained intact until 1865, when the house and its beautiful avenues of locust-trees, which Sir Peter had planted with his own hand, were levelled to make way for a row of brick dwellings. The remainder of the estate, at the time of its partition, was divided up into holdings of twelve or fifteen acres, and roads were cut through them which took the names of Sir Peter's daughters. The present Christopher Street was long known as Skinner Road. The Fitzroy Road paralleled the line of the present Eighth Avenue from Fourteenth to Forty-second Street. The Abingdon Road (later Love Lane), on the line of Twenty-first Street, connected what is now Broadway with the Fitzroy Road; while the Southampton Road ran from the present Gansevoort Street to a point on the Abingdon Road a little east of Sixth Avenue. Abingdon Square is the only survival of these family names.

Sir Peter was not without neighbors of quality during his residence in Greenwich. Other rich men soon elected to keep him company, and the country-seats clustered about his own included before 1767 those of William Bayard, James Jauncey, and Lady Warren's brother, Oliver De Lancey, whose loyalty to the crown during the Revolution cost him his estates. The residence there of such elegant people was sure to be remembered by their friends in the city when on pleasure bent, and thus a drive to Greenwich became, during the later colonial period, one of the favorite recreations of fashionable folk. The water-side road to the village, along the line of Greenwich Street, crossed Lispenard's Meadows and Minetta Water, and was often heavy after a rain or a strong spring tide; and so, for the greater convenience of Greenwich dwellers and their friends, in 1768 a lane was opened from the Bowery westward across the fields. Astor Place and Greenwich Avenue are surviving sections of this lane, which was called also Monument or Obelisk Lane, for the reason that at its northern end, near the present intersection of Eighth Avenue and Fifteenth Street, stood a monument in honor of General Wolfe.

Townsfolk taking the air in the old days usually made this monument the objective point of an afternoon drive, thence returning homeward by way of the Southampton Road and the riverside. Time, which makes an end of all things, long since claimed both lane and obelisk. The execution of the City Plan spared only the aforesaid remnants of the former, while the memorial to the hero of Quebec disappeared during the British occupation of New York in Revolutionary times, and sixscore years of searching has revealed no trace of it. Those who busy themselves with the minor points of history incline to the belief that it was either buried or shipped out of the country by English soldiers, who feared harm might come to it if left to the keeping of a nation of rebels.

Before the opening of Greenwich Lane the village which gave it a name had thrown out two off-shoots. One of these, known as Lower Greenwich, lay at the foot of Brannan (now Spring) Street, while Upper Greenwich nestled at the foot of what is now Christopher Street and then was the Skinner Road. Traces of the latter remain in a row of low wooden houses on West Street, between Christopher and Tenth, but best seen from Weehawken Street, in the rear. These houses were standing prior to 1767, and are among the oldest on the Island of Manhattan. The Revolution brought no material change to

HOUSES IN WEEHAWKEN STREET, GREENWICH VILLAGE—THE OLDEST BUILDINGS NOW STANDING IN NEW YORK

Greenwich, and the next important event in its history fell in 1796, when a State prison was built in the upper village. The prison stood at the foot of Tenth (then Amos) Street, and portions of its walls are incorporated with those of the brewery that now occupies the site. The prison-yard reached down to the water, and outside of the high stone wall enclosing it lay open fields and a wide stretch of beach. Now streets ending in piers have been extended west of the prison site and far into the river.

The prison continued in use until Sing Sing superseded it in 1828, when the property passed by sale into private hands. Greenwich folk no doubt rejoiced at its passing, for its history had been thickly strewn with revolts among the prisoners. The first of these, in 1799, was only quelled when the guards opened fire on half a hundred convicts and wounded several of them. In 1803 another band of mutineers fired the prison and, escaping into the yard, tried to scale the walls, but were reduced to submission after the shooting of the ring-leaders. Again, in 1804, the keepers were overpowered and locked in the north wing of the prison, which was then fired. One more humane than the rest released them before the wing was consumed, but in the confusion many of the prisoners succeeded in making their escape.

Greenwich people, despite these outbreaks, appear to have counted the prison one of the attractions of their town. The manager of the Greenwich Hotel advertises, in September, 1811, that "a few gentlemen may be accommodated with board and lodging at this pleasant and healthy situation, a few doors from the State Prison;" and he adds that "the Greenwich stage passes from this to the Federal Hall and returns five times a day." Greenwich was growing apace when this advertisement appeared in the *Columbian.* Five years later Asa Hall's line of stages was established, with departures from Greenwich on the even hours and from the corner of Broadway and Pine Street on the uneven ones. The fare each way was twenty-five cents, and the stages ran all day, their arrival and departure being heralded by the blowing of a horn. Kipp's stages, at a yet later period, started from the corner of Pine and Nassau Streets, passed up Broadway to Canal, and thence made their way, past farms and gardens, to Greenwich. Genial and warm-hearted Sol Kipp was long the life and soul of the village, and Dayton writes that "in fun or frolic he was on hand, well knowing that his bright face and white cravat would receive a hearty welcome in any gathering of his fellows. Ample means seemed ever at his command to gratify a wish or relieve a friend in distress, and it was not until the projection of horse-cars along the line of his remunerative route that misfortune overtook him. He battled for years in the courts against the starting of the Eighth Avenue Railroad, but finally succumbed before the power of George Law and his millions," and in friendless age went out of life as poor as he had entered it.

Tom Paine ended his stormy career as a resident of Greenwich, and John Randel, Junior, engineer to the commissioners by whom was prepared the present City Plan, has left a quaint record of the author of "The Age of Reason" as he appeared in his last days. The commissioners then had their office at the corner of Christopher and Herring (now Bleecker) Street. "I boarded in the city," writes Randel, "and in going to the office almost daily passed the house in Herring Street (now No. 293 Bleecker) where Thomas Paine resided, and frequently in fair weather saw him sitting at the south window of the first-story room of that house. The sash was raised, and a small table or stand was placed before him with an open book upon it which he appeared to be reading. He had his spectacles on, his left elbow rested upon the table or stand, and his chin rested between the thumb and fingers of his hand; his right hand lay upon his book, and a decanter containing liquor of the color of rum or brandy was standing next his book or beyond it. I never saw Thomas Paine at any other place or in any other position."

A long and thorny road led Paine to a final refuge in Greenwich Village. When he came from England to America, in 1774, his Quaker ancestry and training and the letters from Franklin which he brought with him induced his settlement in Philadelphia. There he became the editor of the *Pennsylvania Magazine,* leaped at once into public notice as a vigorous advocate of liberty, and at the end of a twelvemonth published his famous "Common Sense." This pamphlet was a clarion call for separation from England, and so radical was its influence on the wavering colonies that Edmund Randolph, a devout churchman, writing long after the author's death, ascribed American independence primarily to George III. and next to Thomas Paine. Half a million copies of "Common Sense" were sold, the proceeds of which the author devoted to the cause of independence, thus, as the price was two shillings a copy, giving away a fortune in this pamphlet alone. A little later he also bestowed upon his adopted country the copyright of his "Crisis," and ate his crust contentedly, "peace finding him a penniless patriot who might easily have had fifty thousand pounds in his pocket."

Paine, moreover, was a man of action as well as of words. While the Declaration of Independence was signing he abandoned his magazine, and marched with his musket to the front, serving first in a Pennsylvania division of the Flying Camp under General Roberdeau, and then as volunteer aide-de-camp on the staff of General Greene. It was when Washington's distressed and discomforted army had reached Newark that he began to write his magical "Crisis," the first thrilling words of which, falling on the ears of the half-clad soldiers, were in themselves a victory. "These are the times that try men's souls!" Rallying to the onset with such a watchword, the battle of Trenton was won.

Nor was Paine's after-service to the patriot cause less weighty and important. In May, 1780, by the timely suggestion of a subscription, which he headed with five hundred dollars of his scant salary as clerk of the Pennsylvania Assembly, in answer to Washington's gloomiest appeal from Morristown, he started a popular movement, resulting in the subscription of three hundred thousand pounds, and thus establishing the bank that supplied the army throughout the campaign. The following year he went abroad with Colonel Laurens, and secured from the French king a gift of six million dollars. For this service, the plan of which was conceived and mainly executed by him, he never received payment or even acknowledgment. Laurens, who bungled the delicate mission, got the glory and the pay; Paine, who had run the greater danger and done the work, got nothing. Worse still, when the war was over and lesser heroes were liberally rewarded with place and power, Congress voted Paine a paltry three thousand dollars, and only two States remembered him,—Pennsylvania with a gift of two thousand five hundred dollars and New York with a farm at New Rochelle.

Paine sailed for Europe in 1787, and not until 1802 did he return to America. During the intervening years he had been outlawed by England and imprisoned by France, but had given to the world his "Rights of Man" and "Age of Reason." When, at the age of sixty-two, he came again to the nation he had helped to create, he was met by the new faces of a generation that knew him not, and by the cold shoulders, instead of the outstretched hands, of old friends. This was the bitter fruit of his "Age of Reason," which remains of all epoch-making books the one most persistently misquoted and misunderstood; for even now there are those who rate it as scoffing and scurrilous, whereas its tone throughout is noble and reverent, and some of the doctrines which it teaches are now recognized as not inimical to religion. It does not require in a more tolerant age a high order of courage to write these words; but less than a hundred years ago there ruled in America a spirit of narrow and militant bigotry; and from his arrival in Baltimore until his death, seven years later, Paine was subjected to constant and virulent abuse. One fanatic even tried to kill him; and in 1806 he was denied the right to vote at his home in New Rochelle,—disfranchised in the country to which he had rendered services pronounced pre-eminent by Washington and by every soldier and statesman of his time.

Paine passed his closing years on his farm at New Rochelle, often in want, but never a stranger to self-respect, and occupied to the last with thoughts of political and religious liberty. His health began to fail in 1808, and then it was that he found lodging in the Greenwich house where Randel saw him. Towards the end, in order to make him more comfortable than was possible in a lodging-house, his friend Madame Bonneville hired a small frame dwelling near that in which they were then living, and removed him thither. This house stood at what is now No. 59 Grove Street, and within its walls Paine died on June 8, 1809, neglected and unmourned. Aside from Madame Bonneville and her children, only three persons, two negroes and a Quaker preacher, Willett Hicks,—let his name be honored!—accompanied the body to the grave beyond New Rochelle. A monument, erected by a later and more grateful generation, now marks the spot, but not the present resting-place of his remains. William Cobbett took them to England in 1818, and where they were finally buried remains a mystery. Barrow Street was once known as Raisin Street, a corruption of Reason Street, the name originally given it by the authors of the City Plan in compliment to Paine, their neighbor in Greenwich for more than a year.

Greenwich, by reason of its healthfulness and location, early became a refuge for the people of New York in time of pestilence. A letter from Lieutenant-Governor Clarke to the Duke of Newcastle, dated April 18, 1739, begs leave "to inform your Grace that the Small Pox being in town, and one third of the Assembly not having had it, I gave them leave to sit at Greenwich;" and whenever, in after years, yellow fever raged in the town, there was sure to be a general exodus to the village beyond Lispenard's Meadows. "As soon as this dreadful scourge makes its appearance in New York," wrote John Lambert, in 1807, "the inhabitants shut up their shops and fly from their houses into the country. Those who cannot go far, on account of business, remove to Greenwich, situate on the border of the Hudson River about two or three miles from town. Here the merchants and others have their offices, and carry on their concerns with little danger from the fever, which does not seem to be contagious beyond a certain distance. The banks and other public offices also remove their business to this place; and markets are regularly established for the supply of the inhabitants." Lambert adds that in 1805 upward of twenty thousand people fled from the city.

Again, in 1822, when the fever claimed an army of victims in the town, Greenwich was crowded with panic-stricken refugees. "Saturday, the 24th of August," writes Hardie, "our city presented the appearance of a town besieged. From daybreak till night one line of carts, containing boxes, merchandise, and effects, was seen moving towards Greenwich Village and the upper parts of the city. Carriages and hacks, wagons and horsemen, were scouring the streets and filling the roads; persons with anxiety strongly marked on their countenances, and with hurried gait, were hustling through the streets. Temporary stores and offices were erecting, and even on the ensuing day (Sunday) carts were in motion, and the saw and hammer busily at work. Within a few days thereafter the custom-house, the post-office, the banks, the insurance offices, and the printers of newspapers located themselves in the village or in the upper part of Broadway, where they were free from the impending danger; and these places almost instantaneously became the seat of the immense business usually carried on in the great metropolis." The Brooklyn ferry-boats ran regularly to Greenwich, and blocks of business structures were reared almost in a day. Another eye-witness relates that on a Saturday morning he saw corn growing on the present corner of West

Eleventh and Fourth Streets, and on Monday found the site occupied by a house capable of accommodating three hundred lodgers.

A majority of the refugees returned to the city when the fever had spent its force, but many found homes in Greenwich, which a little later ceased to be a detached village and became a suburb of the growing town. Its final surrender, however, was a conditional one. The lanes which grew into roads and then into streets while it was yet a village still follow their ancient course, and hitched to the most readily available streets in the City Plan bid defiance to the rectangular lines of that rigid instrument. Fourth Street crosses Tenth, Eleventh, and Twelfth Streets very nearly at right angles, and a score of like anomalies serve to recall the loose and easy ways of an earlier day. A yet more impressive reminder of olden times is the tiny graveyard at the corner of Eleventh Street and Sixth Avenue,—what remains of the second cemetery owned on the Island of Manhattan by the Jews. The first Beth Haim, opened in 1681, in what is now the New Bowery, was closed early in the last century, and the Beth Haim at Greenwich purchased by the Congregation of Sharith Israel. But when Eleventh Street was opened in 1830 on the lines of the City Plan, it cut directly across this second burial-ground, leaving only the corner on the south side, and a still smaller corner on the north side.

When Greenwich was still a village and Monument Lane a shaded country road, what is now Washington Square was a potter's field. Besides serving that purpose for many years after 1797, it was used as a place of execution, and the writer has talked with old gentlemen who recall the time when the gallows set up near the present Washington Arch kept grim vigil over the pauper graves around it. Washington Square while still a potter's field was the scene of at least one duel with a fatal ending. William Coleman founded the *Evening Post* in 1801, and from the first made it an aggressive advocate of Federalist principles. Political feeling ran high in those days, and it was not long before he became embroiled with the leading Republican editor of the town,—James Cheetham, of the *American Citizen*. Coleman was challenged by Cheetham, and, friends having failed to settle the difficulty, Judge Brockholst Livingston, to prevent a meeting, caused the arrest of the two editors. When one Thompson, a friend of Cheetham, declared that Coleman "had shown the white feather," Coleman's friends insisted that he challenge Thompson. He yielded to their urging, and, his challenge having been accepted, plans for a meeting were laid with great secrecy.

Dr. McLean, a well-known surgeon, received an anonymous letter to the effect that he would find at nine o'clock, the evening of its date, a horse and gig on the south side of the Bowling Green. He was to take it and drive to the point where Greenwich Lane skirted the potter's field. He did as requested, and reached the point in time to hear pistol shots and to see by the light of the moon one man supporting another, while two others stood close at hand. The doctor was told that the wounded man needed aid, and should be placed in charge of his friends. Then the speaker, who was no other than Cheetham, laid the wounded man on the ground, and disappeared in the direction already taken by Coleman and his second. McLean found the sufferer to be Thompson, stanched the blood flowing from his side, carried him to his home, and, placing him at the door, rang the bell, and departed before the family had answered the summons. Thompson, declaring he had been honorably treated, refused to disclose the name of his antagonist or to give any account of the affair. He died of his wound on the second day, and Coleman went unpunished.

The University of New York has now found an abiding-place beyond the Harlem, but glorious memories cling to its first home,—the gray-stone structure which stood from 1830 to 1894 on the east side of Washington Square, growing more venerable and picturesque with each passing year. Theodore Winthrop, soon to fall at Big Bethel, lodged within the walls of the now vanished building when he wrote his "Cecil Dreeme," and so did Samuel Colt when working out the idea of the revolver. Science also has memories of the place. Samuel F. B. Morse had rooms there in 1835, and, with crude apparatus made by his own hand, gave the first exhibition of telegraphy to his art pupils. Afterwards he secured better instruments, and strung his wires from the university to a hotel across the square, at the corner of Thompson Street. His old instruments are still preserved in the University museum. While Morse was working at the telegraph, John W. Draper had his laboratory in another part of the building. There he experimented with nitrate of silver until he was ready to take pictures, when he went with his sister to the roof, where she sat for half an hour before his camera. Then putting the plate in his fixing-baths, he succeeded in making the first permanent photograph of the human face. Draper's son Henry afterwards lived in the building, and there won fame by his photographs of the moon.

Commodore Vanderbilt long had his home at No. 10 Washington Place, and George William Curtis resided on Washington Square during the early years of his fruitful and many-sided career. The house numbered 21 Washington Place was for several years the home of the elder Henry James, and there his son and namesake entered life; while in adjacent Waverly Place stands the dwelling, recently rebuilt, in which Anne Lynch, afterwards Mrs. Botta, began the receptions which until her death continued to be a distinctive feature of the literary life of New York. Charles Fenno Hoffman dwelt in Greene Street before he passed into the mental gloom that clouded his remaining years; Bayard Taylor lived in University Place when he wrote his "Masque of the Gods," and near-by Clinton Place is associated with the name and labors of Evert A. Duyckinck. The erstwhile homes of these authors have been swept away;

but one literary landmark of Greenwich Village is yet spared to the lover of the past, for what is now the parish-house of St. Luke's Church in Hudson Street was the boyhood home of Bret Harte, and thence he set forth upon the wanderings which made him one of the New World Argonauts whom his genius has clothed with undying romance.

X

Chelsea & Love Lane

A FEW years after Captain Warren and his American wife took up their residence in Greenwich Village, that is about 1750, Captain Thomas Clarke, a veteran of the provincial service, with a long record of hard fighting in the old French War, went still farther afield, and bought an estate on the shores of the Hudson, some three miles north of the town of New York, to which he gave the name of Chelsea, after the well-known hospital near London, and as one befitting the home of an old soldier in the evening of his days. The captain, however, did not long enjoy the peace and quiet of his waterside retreat. His home was burned to the ground during his last illness, and he died in a near-by farm-house, where he had been carried by rescuing neighbors.

Mistress Molly Clarke, the captain's widow, becomingly mourned her loss, and then, being a woman of spirit and enterprise, set herself to the work of rebuilding. The house she built, a large, square, two-storied structure, stood upon the crest of a low hill, not far from the riverside, some two hundred feet west of the present Ninth Avenue, and with one of its corners on the southern line of Twenty-third Street. There she lived for many years, and in 1802 died at a ripe old age, having witnessed greater changes than fall to the lot of most women. That part of her estate which extended from Eighth Avenue and Nineteenth Street to Twenty-fourth Street and the Hudson then passed, with the homestead, to Bishop Benjamin Moore, who had married her daughter, and from him it descended in 1813 to his only son, Clement C. Moore. The younger Moore added another story to the old house, and it stood until 1853, with its terraced grounds shaded by oaks and elms, a picturesque survival of the past. But when, to quote the words of its owner, " the corporation of the city ordered a bulkhead to be built along the river-front," it was thought advisable, if not absolutely necessary, to dig down the whole place and throw it into the river, when, of course, the old house was destroyed. Now a row of brick buildings occupies its site.

Clement C. Moore, like his father before him, was, according to all testimony, a man of beautifully rounded character, and in widely varied ways made a distinct impression on his time. He was fitted for the ministry, after being graduated at Columbia in 1798, but he never took orders, devoting himself instead to Oriental and classical studies. Mines, speaking with the authority of long friendship, describes him as the kindliest of scholars, the most assiduous of bookworms, a writer whose works were held in highest regard by the learned men of his day. Yet Moore is known to posterity by none of these things. It was his custom to employ his leisure in writing verse, not for profit or publication, but to lighten his severer labors; and it was "A Visit from St. Nicholas," written solely to amuse his children that made his name a household word. This nursery-rhyme, so dear to the heart of childhood, was written in 1822. A young lady visiting the family copied it into her album, and sent it, unknown to Dr. Moore, to the editor of the Troy *Sentinel,* who printed it at Christmas-time of the following year. Thence it found its way into the school-readers, and by this modest pathway its author mounted up to fame. Nothing he has written survives except this poem, which he counted of slight literary merit.

Dr. Moore was a man of affairs as well as a

scholar and maker of verse. A few years after the Chelsea estate came into his possession he began opening through it the existing streets and avenues on the lines of the City Plan, and thereafter gave much time and energy to fostering the growth of the village which he founded upon his lands. Rows of dwellings, known as the London Terrace and Chelsea Cottages, were soon built, the one in Twenty-third and the other in Twenty-fourth Street, and still exist to recall the time when their pilastered fronts and deep gardens caused them to be much sought after by people who wished to combine the comforts of the town with the quiet of the countryside. At the time of their building, in 1845, Chelsea had been for a score of years the seat of the General Theological Seminary of the Episcopal Church. Dr. Moore, who was one of its professors from 1821 until his death, gave this institution rent-free the whole of the block between Twentieth and Twenty-first Streets and Ninth and Tenth Avenues, and this area of about sixty lots, being for many years only in small part built upon, was long known as Chelsea Square. Here the East Building of the Seminary was erected in 1825, and the West Building ten years later. Both of these structures, with the minor edifices that in time grew up about them, were of dark graystone, and with their ivy-clad walls, set off by greensward and a wealth of embowering shade, gave to Chelsea Square half a century ago the appearance of a section of an English university town. All of these stone buildings save one have now given way to wide-spreading piles of brick, but a goodly portion of the square has been spared by the builder, and its lawns and trees and flower-beds make it one of the most satisfying prospects to be had in an afternoon stroll around the Island of Manhattan.

St. Peter's Episcopal Church, in West Twentieth Street between Eighth and Ninth Avenues, and the Church of the Holy Apostles, at the corner of West Twenty-eighth Street and Ninth Avenue, also carry one back to the time when the roads of Chelsea Village were first giving place to city streets. St. Peter's, a graystone structure with a tall and massive tower, was erected in 1836, and during its sixty-six years of existence has undergone fewer changes than has been the lot of most New York churches. Old Chelsea families are still represented in the vestry, and the scholarly repose of Chelsea Square on the opposite side of the way preserves in its surroundings something of the quiet which rested upon them before Chelsea became a part of the city. The Church of the Holy Apostles belongs to a slightly more recent period, but behind its building lies a story full of human interest. "A young man, son of a great ship-builder," we are told, "determined to study for the ministry of the Episcopal Church, though his father was not of that faith. The son persisted, and the father made his will, cutting off the disobedient son with the proverbial shilling. Ordained and in the ministry, but cut off from the wealth he should have inherited, the son kept on his way unmoved, but not unwatched by the father. Touched by his consistent conduct, the father made a new will, leaving him his entire possessions. Then the old man died. The son divided the property equally among the heirs, and out of his own share built the Church of the Holy Apostles as a thank-offering."

Dr. Moore died in 1863, but it is only within the present year (1902) that his estate was divided among his heirs. Another large owner of land in Chelsea, though of a subsequent period, was Don Alonzo Cushman, whose spacious grounds and hospitable residence in Ninth Avenue opposite the Theological Seminary remained until 1896 a conspicuous feature of the district. Cushman came to New York from Coventry, Connecticut, in 1810, and took a clerkship in a dry-goods house. By 1830 he had prospered sufficiently to purchase the site in Chelsea whereon he built a home; and subsequent purchases made him the owner of an estate that comprised the east and west sides of Ninth Avenue from Nineteenth to Twenty-first Streets; and the south side of Twenty-third Street from Ninth Avenue half-way to Eighth Avenue, and also from Ninth Avenue to Tenth Avenue. The value of this estate at his death, in 1871, was estimated at three and a half millions, but when a final division among his heirs was made a few years ago it had increased to double that sum.

When Cushman took up his residence in Chelsea, to reach the city a stage trip was necessary through the village of Greenwich, while the garden of his homestead bordered on Love Lane, which ran from the Bloomingdale Road (the present Broadway) to the Hudson, close on the line of what is now Twenty-first Street. Love Lane, known also as the Abingdon Road, long since surrendered to the City Plan, but more than one interesting trace survives to reward the searcher after tokens of the past. The two-storied brick houses lately gone from 53 and

55 West Twenty-first Streets stood at the point where of old the Southampton Road came into Love Lane, and at least one authority holds to the belief that originally they were a single house which served as a road-side tavern. Again, west of Sixth Avenue, a large open space on the south side of the way bears silent witness to the time when Love Lane ran through a quiet countryside. It is the Jewish graveyard established here when, seventy odd years ago, the one at Greenwich was practically swept away by the opening of Eleventh Street. A high wall hides it from view, and there have been no burials within its confines since the Beth Haim was opened on Long Island a generation or more ago; but its graves are garlanded every summer with flowers, and the care given to its gravelled walks and time-worn headstones show that those who sleep there are not forgotten.

Before it was carried eastward to the Hudson, some time prior to 1811, Love Lane ended at the Fitzroy Road, which, as we know, ran from a point a little south of the present Fifteenth to Forty-second Street, close upon the line of Eighth Avenue. The Fitzroy Road was long since superseded by the streets of the City Plan, but traces of it reward the quest of the patient seeker. A section of it remains in use in the drive-way to a brewery at Eighteenth Street, and a block below another section has become a court running into the centre of the block.

The Fitzroy Road merged into the Southampton Road near the present Fifteenth Street, and of the latter there survives a signally curious remnant in the group of wooden houses buried in the heart of the block between Sixteenth and Seventeenth Streets and Sixth and Seventh Avenues, and once known as Paisley Place, or the Weaver's Row. Eighty years ago hand-weaving was still a thriving industry, and Paisley Place got its name and being from a company of Scotch weavers who settled there during the yellow-fever epidemic of 1822. "At a little distance from where the large merchants had their homes," writes P. M. Wetmore, referring to Greenwich Village, "ran a secluded country lane which bore the somewhat pretentious name of Southampton Road. A convenient nook by the side of this quiet lane was chosen by a considerable number of Scotch weavers as their place of refuge from the impending danger. They erected their modest dwellings in a row, set up their frames, spread their webs, and the shuttles flew merrily from willing fingers. With the love of Scotland strong in their hearts and the old town from which they had wandered warm in their memories, they gave their new home the name of Paisley Place." The Scotch weavers are gone, but the houses which they built still hold their long-accustomed place on the line of the vanished Southampton Road, while of the scattered village which, with Paisley as its nucleus, grew up between Greenwich and Chelsea threescore years ago there survived until a very recent period a marked and interesting feature in the two wooden houses with outside stairs leading to the second story which stood in what once were gardens at Nos. 251 and 253 West Eighteenth Street, and whose quaintness was of a sort to warm the heart of the antiquarian.

From Paisley Place the Southampton Road bore away across country by the east and north, and following its ancient course to the end we come again to Love Lane, where, after its surrender to the City Plan, George Bancroft for many years had his home. During the year 1849 Bancroft's address was No. 32, but thereafter, until 1867, the directory placed him at No. 17 West Twenty-first Street. In the third story of this house he placed the literary gatherings of many years, and there wrought upon the imposing history which furnishes his strongest claim to remembrance. It is recorded that he chose New York as a residence because he thought it pleasanter than all other places; and it is also recorded that in his loyalty to his native New England he once said that New York was an encampment of dollar-hunters, with few scholars. Be this as it may, Bancroft had the genius for making friends of men and women of like mind and cultivation, and for nearly a score of years at his New York home were met more cultured and eminent people than at any other one house in the city. He left New York in 1867 to become minister to Prussia. When he returned to America, in 1874, he took up his residence in Washington, and in that city and at Newport he spent his later years.

A three-story brick building at No. 35 East Nineteenth Street was the last city home of Horace Greeley. Here the founder of the *Tribune* and his daughters dwelt for many years, when around the corner in East Twentieth Street lived the sisters Cary. The modest home of these gifted women has changed but little since it passed into the hands of strangers. In the small bay-windowed parlor on the ground floor were held the Sunday night receptions which long had for regular attendants the city's choicest spirits. Phœbe Cary's study was directly above the parlor, and in an adjoining room her sister Alice wrote some of her best verse, and there laid down her pen forever.

An apartment-house has replaced, at No. 136 West Twentieth Street, the last home of General Winfield Scott; but the house at No. 436 West Twenty-second Street, in which Edwin Forrest once lived, stands very much as he left it, even as to its interior and furniture. Here the tragedian and his English wife, Catherine Sinclair, dwelt for several years, holding receptions at which Bryant, Willis, and other notable men were frequent guests; and here occurred the sudden mysterious quarrel ending in the divorce case that helped to make the fame of Charles O'Conor. It is a wide-front dwelling of brick, two stories and a basement, with a mansard roof that is really a third story. The entrance is by a broad stone staircase, set near the centre of the front. When Forrest bought the property it had a big garden in the rear, which is still there, fenced about with ornamental walls of wood, decked in these later days with a profusion of trailing vines and greenery. Tradition has it that the property passed to the actor from

PORCHES AND GARDEN, EDWIN FORREST HOUSE, NO. 436 WEST TWENTY-SECOND STREET

a wealthy Englishman, who built it as the exact counterpart of the girlhood home of his wife, designing thus to cure the home-sickness to which she had fallen a victim.

It has been the home for many years of a wealthy retired merchant, who, with a love for antiques and ample means for its gratification, has gathered there one of the choice art collections of the town, making it a storehouse literally overflowing with objects as costly and curious as they are rare and beautiful. Every inch of wall in the house is covered with works of art, and the old-fashioned spiral staircase, so often referred to by witnesses in the famous divorce trial, is decked with rugs and tapestries. A fortune has been expended on ivory carvings, displayed in cabinets of the time of Louis XV., and there are rare old bronzes, quaint andirons, and costly porcelains.

Richly embroidered chairs from the castle at Fontainebleau are grouped around the open fireplace, and the north wall of the reception-parlor is crowded with fine old miniatures. Two photographs in oval silver frames hang on the eastern wall. They are portraits of Forrest and his wife. The actor's face has an amiable expression not found in his other photographs. The owner spent years in patient search before he secured the picture of Mrs. Forrest, which represents her in her youth, when she was famed for her beauty. Time-pieces of by-gone days, including both clocks and watches, are hung on the southern wall, over a satin-lined case filled with lotus-leaf carvings in ivory. A noteworthy feature of the dining-room is a tall cabinet containing a complete dinner-set which Louis Philippe once used at the Tuileries and which bears the royal crest. Old silver fills other cabinets in the hall-way outside, and oil-paintings, antique swords, and ancient armor adorn the walls of the stairway. When the owner could no longer find room for his treasures in the house itself he went out to the porch and garden beyond, placing them among the plants and flowers, and filling the porch with armor, lanterns, wood-carvings, and rare rugs. On this porch Forrest used to sit on summer evenings and sip, in the intervals of pleasant familiar talk, the then novel and delicious mint-juleps that his wife brewed for him and his friends, and of which he was very fond. Books are stored on the second floor of the house, where Forrest had his library; and the top story, where were his wardrobe and dressing-room, has become a bachelor's den and library where the present owner's son passes his leisure hours. All in all the old home of Forrest is a curiously beautiful house, made interesting not alone by past associations, but also by the patient zeal which has wrought its present adornment.

Thence a short stroll leads on to the site at the southeast corner of Twenty-third Street and Sixth Avenue of the theatre erected by Edwin Booth. This massive and beautiful structure was designed by its builder as a permanent home of the legitimate drama, and its opening on February 3, 1869, was an incident that holds an abiding-place in the memory of veteran theatre-goers. There during a period of four years Booth was seen in productions of "Romeo and Juliet," "Othello," "Hamlet," "The Lady of Lyons," "Richelieu," "Much Ado About Nothing," "The Fool's Revenge," "A Winter's Tale," and "Julius Cæsar," in the last named representing at different times Brutus, Cassius, and Antony. All of these dramas were revived by a well-balanced company and with a splendor of scenes and dresses beyond precedent in the history of the stage. But the richness and beauty of its appointments, coupled with bad management, in the end wrought the ruin of Booth's Theatre. Booth left it in June,

1873, and in February following his bankruptcy was declared, when the theatre finally passed out of his control. It was subsequently managed by Junius Brutus Booth, by Jarrett & Palmer, by Augustin Daly, and by others who strove in vain to establish it in public favor. It was finally closed on April 30, 1883, with a memorable performance of "Romeo and Juliet," the same play with which it had opened, and soon afterwards it was demolished. Edwin Booth continued to act for eighteen years after the failure of the theatre which bore his name, and in which his hopes were centred, and by his art accumulated a large fortune, part of which he devoted in his last days to the purchase of the building No. 16 Gramercy Park as a home for the Player's Club instituted by him.

This famous actor took what proved to be his farewell of the stage at the Academy of Music, Brooklyn, on April 4, 1891, and two years later he died. The memory of him that endures is not only that of the most gifted player of his time, but also of one of the gentlest and most generous of men, and by those who knew and loved him a hundred proofs are given of his kindness of heart, delicacy of feeling, and unbounded silent charity. When an old friend and fellow-player died, writes Lawrence Hutton, " Booth bought a lot for his remains, buried him, placed a handsome monument over his head, purchased a house and furnished it fully for the widow, and gave her a liberal income, continued to her after his own death. Another old friend of Booth, a superannuated actor, and a very aged man, lunched with him one day at the Players. The weather was threatening as he left, and his host sent him home in a carriage. The guest was very much affected when they parted and tried to say something, in a half-tearful way, which Booth would not let him utter. After he had gone some one spoke of the gentleness and sweetness of the veteran's character, and said it was to be hoped that he had managed to save enough to keep his body and soul together for the little time that was left to him here. 'Oh, yes; he's all right!' replied Booth. 'He has something to support him comfortably as long as he lives; and I am glad of it.' After Booth had passed away it was learned that the something was furnished by Booth, who had invested nine thousand dollars in an annuity to cheer his fellow-player's declining years. But he did not even hint of such a deed."

A block from the site of Booth's Theatre, and

on the opposite side of the way, stands the Fifth Avenue Hotel, built by Amos R. Eno between 1856 and 1859, and for New York, therefore, an old hotel. Its site was occupied in an earlier time by a road-house, a small wooden building with a piazza running across the front, known as Corporal Thompson's Madison Cottage, and the last stopping-place of pleasure-seekers returning to town by way of the Bloomingdale Road. Franconi's Imperial Hippodrome was afterwards built there, and was still standing when Eno became the owner of the property. He bought other land than this, and upon a plot owned by him in West Twenty-fourth Street, just out of Broadway, a building was erected during the Civil War period for business purposes, but passing soon into the hands of James Fiske, was by him transformed into the Fifth Avenue Theatre.

Fiske chose John Brougham as his manager, but ere long quarrelled with him and dispensed with his services. Then Augustin Daly, securing a lease of the theatre, there revealed his remarkable capacity as a manager; and when checked by the accident of fire in 1873, carried the name of the Fifth Avenue to Twenty-eighth Street, and set up his dramatic fortunes in a new building. The burned theatre was rebuilt within the same year, and early in 1880 passed to the control of the Mallory Brothers, publishers of the *Churchman,* who dedicated it to the moral drama under the name of Madison Square. Steele Mackaye's "Hazel Kirke" was their first venture and had one of the longest runs on record, bringing them a fortune. After that Albert M. Palmer purchased a controlling interest in the house, and for several years directed its affairs. Then it became Hoyt's Theatre, and now again bears its old name.

The Fifth Avenue Hotel, when opened to the public in August, 1859, sprang at once into favor, and its old registers bear the names of men and women eminent in every walk of life. King Edward VII., then the Prince of Wales, was one of its early guests. The king's brother-in-law, the Duke of Argyll, was at the hotel later, as were Dom Pedro of Brazil, and Prince Iturbide of Mexico, Maximilian's adopted son. For upward of forty years every President has been registered here, and Lincoln went from the Fifth Avenue to Cooper Union to make the speech that started him on the road to the Presidency. Grant's candidacy for the same office was first discussed at a dinner of the Peabody Fund trustees at the Fifth Avenue in 1867, and he and his cabinet once held an official session at the same place. Roscoe Conkling and General William T. Sherman lived here during their last years; here Garfield and Cleveland held their first receptions and Arthur received the first Corean embassadors. It was also the stopping-place of James G. Blaine when he visited New York, and the scene of the Burchard incident which in 1884 lost him the Presidency.

The post-election fight which won the same office for Hayes had its inception at the Fifth Avenue. Samuel J. Tilden was the Democratic candidate for President in 1876, and he directed his own campaign with shrewdness, system, and splendid command of details. The South was supposed to be surely Democratic, and the battle centred in the doubtful States of New York, New Jersey, Connecticut, and Indiana. One after another of these States on election night swung into line for Tilden. These with the solid South elected him. People went to bed at midnight and considered the fight at an end. But at an early hour next morning Zachariah Chandler, chairman of the Republican National Committee, received an unexpected caller in his room in the Fifth Avenue Hotel. The visitor, John C. Reid, of the New York *Times,* roused the sleeping chairman and went over the ground carefully, counting the electoral vote in each State. Hayes had received one hundred and sixty-six, but one hundred and eighty-five were needed to elect him. Where were the other nineteen votes to come from? South Carolina, Florida, and Louisiana, said Reid, could furnish them. Though claimed by the Democrats, the result there was still in doubt, and in each of these States the Republicans controlled the returning board. Hayes's managers had but to keep their heads and his election was assured. Chandler asked what should be done.

"Telegraph at once," was the reply, "to leading Republicans, men in authority in the States I have named. Tell them that Hayes is elected if we have carried those States, and to hold them no matter what the odds against them. Then back these men up with the support and resources of the Republican party in the North, and there need be no fears of the result."

The course suggested was instantly adopted, and telegrams, dictated by Reid, were sent off to the three States which were to become the battleground of a new contest for the Presidency. There was no departure during the exciting days that followed from the plan of campaign laid out in Chandler's room in the early morning of November 8, 1876. It is a familiar story of how, in due time, double sets of electoral votes were sent to Congress from Louisiana, Florida, and South Carolina, each certified by rival returning boards, and how the commission created to meet the dilemma decided, but not until two days before the date set for the inauguration of the new President, that these States had cast their electoral votes for Hayes. The quick wit of an editor lost Tilden the Presidency to which he had been elected by a popular majority of two hundred and fifty thousand.

SECTION THREE

BLOOMINGDALE
AND
BEYOND

Old Blue Bell Tavern Kingsbridge Road 1856

XI

Northward from Union Square

THE Bowery of old times was the beginning of the high road to Boston, which, curving first to the right and then to the left, but following in the main the line of the present Third Avenue, ran northward to the Harlem, and crossing that stream passed off the Island of Manhattan. It was, with lower Broadway and the Bowery, for more than a century the only road that traversed the island from end to end, and every turn of the vanished highway is rich in piquant memories of the past.

The lower reaches of the Boston Road have been dealt with in another place, and the stroll here recorded may therefore have its beginning at Union Square. Time was when this square was an unfenced triangle of waste land at the junction of the Boston and Bloomingdale Roads. It became a park when the present City Plan was perfected in 1811, and a little later was flanked by brick and brownstone mansions, whose owners had it planted with trees and fenced in for their exclusive use. That was less than four-score years ago, but now without exception the buildings facing the square have been converted to business purposes, and the only surviving reminder of the time when the region hereabouts was wholly given over to homes is the old Van Beuren mansion in Fourteenth Street, between Fifth and Sixth Avenues, a great house, outwardly plain, with garden and orchard at its skirts, surrounded by shops of every sort and kind. The mansion forms part of the Van Beuren, or, as it is sometimes known, the Spingler estate, which stretches for blocks on every side. Tradition has it that long ago a butcher bought this land, then garden and meadow, and, holding it for half a dozen years, went away to England, leaving it to the care of his apprentice, Henry Spingler by name. The butcher owner never came back, and to the descendants of his apprentice all this estate has come by right of possession; and so valuable is it that it now forms one of the greatest of the great landed estates of Manhattan Island. The original homestead—the present one dates from 1855—was at Fifteenth Street and the Boston Road, and the estate spread east and west and north and south of that point, which was somewhere within the limits of Union Square.

The Academy of Music, at the corner of Fourteenth Street and Irving Place and a little way to the east of the Boston Road, dates from the time when Union Square was still a fashionable place of residence. It was opened in the autumn of 1854 by a company which included Mario and Grisi, and on its stage in the following year occurred the début of Elise Hensler, a native American singer, whose life-story makes romance of the best sort. The daughter of a Boston cobbler, Elise Hensler grew up a handsome brunette, with a superb voice and most engaging manners. Friends, confident of her future, in the course of time supplied the means for a period of study under European masters, and when she made her début at the Academy of Music she met with a most gratifying reception.

Soon afterwards she again crossed the water,

and, following a lengthy residence in Paris, secured an engagement at the royal opera-house in Lisbon. There Don Fernando, consort of Portugal's dead queen and ex-regent of the kingdom, became enamoured of her, had her made court singer, and in 1869 they became husband and wife, Miss Hensler having first accepted the title of Countess of Edla in order that her lover might not marry out of his order. The union proved a most happy one, and Don Fernando's devotion more than once had signal proof. When, in 1869, a delegation of Spanish grandees went about through the royal highways of Europe seeking an occupant for their empty throne, they bethought themselves of the ex-regent of Portugal, who was living quietly at Cintra. "If I accept the throne of Spain, how about my wife?" was his first question when they went to him with their proposition. They said, after some confusion, that she would still be his wife, but not his queen. That settled it, and Don Fernando remained at home. He died in 1885, but his widow still survives, a beautiful, white-haired woman of seventy.

Adelaide Phillips, a singer of English birth, who had been brought to America when a child, and whom the generosity of Jenny Lind had enabled to become the pupil of Manuel Garcia, was first heard at the Academy of Music during the season of 1856; while that of 1859 was remarkable for the appearance in opera of Adelina Patti in the title-rôle of "Lucia di Lammermoor." Mademoiselle Patti was then only sixteen years old, but had already learned to manage her voice, a flute-like flexible soprano, with extraordinary skill and judgment, and capable critics at once hailed her as "one of those rare singers who appear at long intervals to revive not only the hopes of managers but the enthusiasm of the public." This prediction had quick fulfilment. After a short engagement Mademoiselle Patti embarked on a concert tour, which ended at New Orleans, whence she sailed for London, where she may be said to have fairly begun a career which will long remain unique in lyric annals. From her first appearance in the English capital until the present time she has held her position practically undisputed as the greatest of living prima donnas; and to-day, a woman of sixty, she is still a sweeter as well as a better singer than any other in the world.

The season of 1860 brought Clara Louise Kellogg, who was first seen as Gilda in Verdi's "Rigoletto." Three years later on the same stage she conquered complete success by a tender and poetic interpretation of Marguerite in Gounod's "Faust." After that London gave her enthusiastic recognition, and in other characters than Marguerite she was no less successful. In 1869 she again appeared in Italian opera in America, and later for several years headed an English opera company. This organization was the best of its kind formed up to that time, and by stimulating a love of good music exercised a wide-reaching and uplifting influence on public taste. Miss Kellogg's voice was at first a pure and vibrating soprano. It changed as she grew older, losing some of its higher notes, but gaining in strength and richness. She had an excellent method, and all that she did was marked by a fine and pure intelligence. In the power to express with truth and delicacy the highest type of feminine character her equal has not yet appeared among native singers.

The Academy of Music was destroyed by fire in May, 1867, but was at once rebuilt, being reopened in the autumn of the same year with a company which included Minnie Hauk, a young German girl born in New York, who after receiving much encouragement in her native city had gone to Europe to study. She was then only sixteen, and at the close of the season returned to Europe, where for ten years her career was one of steady advancement. In 1878 she came again to New York, and as Carmen in the opera of that name, achieved great and lasting success. A better actress than vocalist, she took the part to herself, and until the coming of Calve there was but one Carmen, and that was Minnie Hauk. The season of 1867 also witnessed the appearance in opera of Euphrosine Parepa, who before that had been heard with acclamation in the concert-room. Her success in opera was no less complete. Parepa's voice was a sweet and brilliant soprano, while her beauty of face and joyousness of spirit helped to win her a secure place in the hearts of those who heard her. Her conductor was always a young German violinist, named Carl Rosa. This gentleman, after a year or two, she kindly took to husband, and in 1872 she went with him to England, where she lived not long, her early death being sincerely mourned by a public which felt that it could better have spared a greater singer.

Among those who appeared at the Academy of Music during the decade following 1871 were Christine Nilsson, a gifted and highly finished vocalist who came heralded as a second Jenny

Lind, but whom those who remembered the older Swedish singer assigned to a slightly lower place; Italo Campanini, one of the best dramatic tenors of his time; Henri Tamberlik, a great tenor and a greater actor; and Emma Albani, who was then quite unknown and unheard of, but who has since won a place among the notable singers of the world. After these came Etelka Gerster, with whom, in November, 1878, Colonel James H. Mapleson, an English impresario of long experience, inaugurated the first of his six seasons of Italian opera at the Academy of Music. Her Majesty's Opera Company, as Mapleson was pleased to style his organization, remained until 1883 the best if not the only interpreter of grand opera in America; but its manager was not to escape the trials and misfortunes that ever wait upon an impresario's life. Many persons who wished places at the Academy of Music were unable to get them on account of the limited number of boxes, and this led to the establishment of the Metropolitan Opera-House, which was opened in October, 1883, with a company headed by Christine Nilsson. Mapleson brought forward Patti as his chief attraction; but the rivalry thus instituted soon made it clear that New York could not support two operatic establishments of magnitude, and at both houses the season ended prematurely in debt, disaster, and confusion. The Academy of Music ceased with its close to be a home of opera, and has since been devoted to spectacular dramas.

Six blocks to the northward, and on the line of the old post-road, lies Gramercy Park, bearing the name by which it was known long before the Revolution. Sixscore years ago the present park was part of a twenty-acre farm owned by James Duane and called Gramercy Seat. The Duane farm, which fronted on the Bloomingdale Road and extended across the Boston Road to a point between Second and Third Avenues, took its name from a creek known as Crummassie-Vly,—Winding Creek,—but later corrupted to Gramercy. This stream, which existed as Cedar Creek until 1845, was fed by several springs in the district between Fifth and Sixth Avenues and Twenty-first and Twenty-seventh Streets, spread out into a pond in passing through the present Madison Square, crossed the Duane farm, and emptied into the East River between Seventeenth and Eighteenth Streets. When, during the Revolution, the British made their attack on the fortifications at Kip's Bay, their Hessian allies simultaneously landed at the mouth of this stream, and, marching westward, encountered a band of patriots, under command of Colonel Samuel Selden, at the junction of the present Third Avenue and Twenty-third Street. Four Hessians were killed in the skirmish which ensued, while Colonel Selden was taken prisoner, to die a few days later of a fever.

James Duane parted with his farm after the Revolution, and at a still later time it passed into the possession of Samuel B. Ruggles, one of the founders of the Bank of Commerce. Ruggles had been active in the movement which made Union Square a fashionable place of residence, and, to induce the erection of first-class dwellings in that locality, he also presented the land for Gramercy Park to the owners of sixty-six adjoining lots, on condition that each lot should be liable for the payment of ten dollars annually, forever, towards a fund designed to plant, preserve, and adorn the projected park. This was in 1831, and the park has preserved until the present time the exclusive character imposed by its founder. The best remembered dweller thereon in later years was Samuel J. Tilden. Cyrus W. Field lived there in an earlier time, with Peter Cooper for neighbor, and there planned the linking of the continents by cable.

The son of a minister, Field was born in the Berkshire Hills in 1819, and when he was fifteen years old came to New York and secured a place in the dry-goods store of Alexander T. Stewart. He began as errand-boy at a dollar a week, but Stewart soon found him to be a lad after his own heart and rapidly advanced him. Before he was twenty-one years old he had saved money enough to go into business for himself. He began in a small way the manufacture and sale of paper, and within a dozen years was at the head of a large business, which enabled him when he was thirty-three years old to retire with a fortune of two hundred and fifty thousand dollars. His real career, however, was still before him, for late in 1853 he was asked to take charge of a project to secure quicker communication between America and Europe, and, consenting to do so, soon found his own future bound up with that of the ocean cable.

Telegraph lines were then being built in many parts of the world, and a Canadian engineer, Gisbourne by name, had projected one between New York and St. John's, Newfoundland, which was to be laid partly on poles, partly under ground, and partly under water. The fastest steamers ever built were to sail from St. John's to the nearest point on the Irish coast, whence other land and water lines were to run to London. It was claimed that in this way a message could be carried from New York to London in six days or less, a considerable saving in time. Gisbourne, however, had built only forty miles of line in Newfoundland when the capitalists acting with him refused to furnish funds for what, on second thought, they had come to regard as a doubtful venture. He thereupon visited New York and asked Matthew D. Field, who was a civil engineer, to aid him in going on with the work. Matthew Field took Gisbourne to his brother Cyrus, and the latter, having listened with interest to what the Canadian had to say, asked for a few days to consider the matter.

Their meeting took place in the library of Field's home on Gramercy Park. After his visitor was gone, he picked up a globe and began to study the relative positions thereon of Newfoundland and Ireland. Suddenly the thought came to him, "Why not a telegraph across the ocean?" This was the germ of the Atlantic cable, but between its conception and realization lay years of heroic struggle. Capital had first to be persuaded, and when this had been accomplished, failure attended both the first and second attempts to lay a cable over sixteen hundred miles of sea-bottom. A third attempt succeeded, and messages were sent from shore to shore. A few days later, however, the messages stopped. Down in the depths of the ocean some fatal mishap had befallen the cable, and the afternoon of success was turned to the bitter night of failure.

The blow fell heaviest on Field, who had risked his entire fortune in the venture. He had no thought, however, of giving up the task. The Civil War delayed his efforts but did not chill his ardor, and before it was ended he was at work again with redoubled energy. The "Great Eastern," the largest vessel afloat, sailed from the Irish coast in July, 1865, only to score another failure,—for after twelve hundred miles of the great rope had sunk into the sea it broke, and the ship put back to England. Again deriders of the enterprise jeered, but not for long. No mishap attended a second voyage on which the "Great Eastern" set forth in the following year. Calm seas kept her company all the way. On July 27, 1866, the American end of the cable was carried into the telegraph house at Heart's Content, and the same day messages were speeding between this country and England.

The "Great Eastern" meantime put back to

mid-ocean to find the cable lost the previous year. It was fished up and spliced, after three weeks of unceasing labor, and safely brought to shore. Both it and its mate are in use to-day, nor since 1866 has there been any serious break in electric communication between the two continents. Not only that, but other men have gone steadily on with the work thus begun, so that now there are upward of one hundred and sixty thousand miles of submarine cables in operation. These bind all of the continents together, and by their use what happens in the morning in some far corner of the Orient is known in the afternoon to the people of New York and Chicago.

A private citizen seldom receives such honors as were showered upon Cyrus W. Field when America and Europe realized that, mainly through his efforts, the continents had been made one. Congress voted him a gold medal with the thanks of the nation, and Great Britain would have done the same had he not been a foreigner. The Paris Exposition of 1867 gave him the Grand Medal, the highest honor at its disposal; the King of Italy bestowed upon him the order of St. Mauritius, and John Bright, in Parliament, called him "the Columbus of modern times, who had moored the new world alongside the old." It is also good to know that the success of the cable restored and added to the fortune he had invested in it. He had subscribed to a fourth of the stock of the cable company, most of which he was unable to sell during the early days of popular distrust of the project, and so,—although he was obliged at one time to pledge his home and library,—when it began to yield large returns to the holders, the fruits of faith in his own idea made him one of the wealthiest men of his period.

Field, however, did not allow his active brain to rest. He lived in New York and loved his city. He studied its wants and saw that its growth depended upon better and quicker ways of getting from one part of the town to another than by the street-car lines then in use. An elevated railroad company had been formed, but had done little. Field secured a majority of the stock and built the roads, and they in turn built the New York of to-day. He was also a leader, as time went on, in other large undertakings; but none of the deeds of his latter years rivalled the great work with which history links his name, and the memory of him which abides in the minds of men—he died in 1892 at the age of seventy-three—is that of one moved through years of doubt and defeat by a faith "before which not a mountain, but the sea was overcome."

Where once was a farm-house beside the Boston Road, and where now is the corner of Madison Avenue and Twenty-sixth Street, stands a silent yet speaking witness to the worth and work of another exceptional man,—the building of the Society for the Prevention of Cruelty to Animals, founded by Henry Bergh. Heir to a fortune, Bergh was educated at Columbia College, and in early manhood served as secretary of the American legation at St. Petersburg. Tarrying in London while on his way home from Russia, he made the acquaintance of the Earl of Harrowby, president of the Royal Society for the Prevention of Cruelty to Animals. This acquaintance grew into friendship, and the young American, becoming deeply interested in the work of the Society, made a careful study of its methods. When he had fully mastered the subject, he returned to New York and founded a similar society, which in the fall of 1864 opened its office at Broadway and Fourth Street.

The Society's modest rooms were furnished with a pine table or two and a few wooden chairs, and its efforts at the outset brought upon its founder the ridicule of the press and the sneers of the crowd; but Bergh persevered, and after a brave fight won for his cause the sympathy and support of the public. He succeeded in having laws passed by the New York Legislature making maltreatment of animals a misdemeanor, and empowering his society to enforce them by means of a staff of officers or special policemen; and thus in the fulness of time he wrought a complete change of sentiment and practice towards animals. Men at first treated their beasts well through fear of arrest; but they soon learned that it paid to be merciful; that by so doing they could get more and better work; and so it has come to pass that animals of all kinds are better treated than ever before in New York, and it is seldom that the officers of the Society have cause to interfere in behalf of their dumb clients. The influence of the movement set afoot by Bergh has not been confined to New York. Humane residents of other cities were early fired by his example, and before his death in 1888 he saw his society grow until it had branches in every portion of the country.

The winning of means for the erection of its present home belongs, however, to the period of its militant and struggling infancy. One day in 1872, when the problem of how to secure money wherewith to carry on his work was still a pressing one, Bergh received a note from a city hospital, asking if he would call upon a patient there, by name Louis Bonnard. He went, and found Bonnard to be a Frenchman, whose business had been for many years that of trapper and fur-trader. The sick man, who lay near to death, described the unnumbered cruelties he had seen practised upon animals during his life among the Indians, and expressed his joy that some one had risen up to be their champion. "You are cool and wise and determined," said he, "and you will go far."

"But I cannot go much farther without help," was Bergh's desponding answer.

"I shall help you," replied the trader. "I have not chased the dollar all these years without catching him now and then. I am a lonely man, and what is mine is mine alone, to do with as I please. Promise me that you will continue in the path upon which you have entered, and what I have shall be at your service."

Bergh gave his promise and went his way, with little thought of the future gift. A few days later, however, word came from the hospital that Bonnard was dead, and had left the Society for the Prevention of Cruelty to Animals his fortune of more than one hundred thousand dollars. And with this noble gift to a noble cause Bergh built a permanent home for his organization, writing in brick and mortar the story of the trader's generous deed.

Four blocks below, at the corner of Fourth Avenue and Twenty-second Street, is the home of the Children's Aid Society, whose founder, Charles Loring Brace, will long be remembered in a city where names go swiftly out of sight, for he was one of those reformers who have drawn attention to vast and neglected evils and led the way to their removal. Born in Hartford in 1826, Brace was graduated at Yale with honor, and studied for the ministry, but at the age of twenty-five he was moved to improve the condition of the vagrant children of the slums, and to this labor, with an unregretting devotion, he gave himself until his death. He was compelled at first to work single-handed and alone, but gradually the way opened before him, and in 1853 a number of influential men in sympathy with his purpose joined him in the organization of the Children's Aid Society.

Brace became the secretary and directing spirit

of the Society, whose mission, though complex and wide-reaching, had yet but a single purpose, —to lift the city's waifs out of their forlorn and often vicious lives and to help them to help themselves. A school of industry and morals adapted to their needs and environment offered the best and least expensive way to accomplish this purpose; and in the section of the city then most given over to vice and misery, in December, 1853, was opened the Fourth Ward Industrial School. The school-room was in the basement of a church in Roosevelt Street. The pupils, the poorest clad and wildest girls of the city, at first seemed wholly uncontrollable, but salaried teachers took them gently in hand, and a number of women who had been induced to join in the undertaking soon had their classes formed and at work. The volunteer teachers, as a rule, took upon themselves the industrial branches, and thanks chiefly to their loving service and patient sacrifice the school proved successful from the very first.

A majority of the pupils, trained to study and industry, and daily brought into familiar contact with refined women, were soon weaned from their former habits and associations. In time nearly all secured places as servants in the city, or situations were found for them in the country. As they grew up they married young mechanics or farmers, and never returned to the class from which they sprang. Encouraged by this first success, and as funds permitted, other schools were opened to pupils of both sexes, too ragged, wild, and irregular to be admitted to the public schools, and now the Society has under its charge more than a score of industrial schools. A majority of them are housed in roomy buildings, erected for the purpose by friends of the society, and each, with slight differences in detail, has duplicated the history of the Fourth Ward School.

The industrial school, however, was not the most important of the helpful agencies early set afoot by Brace and his associates. A newsboys' lodging-house was opened in 1854, and although it was in the loft of the old *Sun* building in Fulton Street, and a small fee was charged each night, it was soon filled with boys who before that had slept in boxes, stairways, and coal-holes in the vicinity of the newspaper offices. When, a little later, "a home in the country" was broached, it met eager welcome from many homeless ones. A party was organized and sent out to Michigan, where places were readily found for the children. This branch of the work grew rapidly, and in all its results was successful beyond the expectations of the most sanguine,—two thousand, and often three thousand, children being sent every year to homes in the country. All the year round the agents of the Society are going from State to State and town to town to pave the way for the coming little ones.

Many of the transplanted waifs have won repute and station. Chief among these, perhaps, is Andrew H. Burke, ex-governor of North Dakota. Forty-odd years ago he was a New York newsboy without home or parents. The Society picked him up and sent him to the West, the party of which he was one going to Nobleville, Ohio, where he found a home with a wealthy man, who sent him to college and gave him a good start in life. Young Burke, after his foster-father's death, removed to Casselton, North Dakota, and became book-keeper in a general store. Six months afterwards he was made cashier of the First National Bank of that place, and a little later treasurer of his county, serving in that capacity until elected governor of North Dakota. "So," he says, writing to the Society in 1891, "the little boy whom you took thirty-three years ago to send to a home in the West is now a full-fledged governor of a sovereign State. Tell your other boys I am proud to have had as humble a beginning as they, and I believe that it has been my salvation. Family name cuts little figure in this country. It is the character of the man that wins recognition."

Charles Loring Brace is dead, but his work lives after him. The last report of the society which he founded states that, aside from its industrial schools and its wide-reaching immigration scheme, it has thirteen night schools, six lodging-houses,—some of them costly buildings and the gifts of individuals,—a farm school at Kensico, a dressmaking and typewriting school, a boys' printing-shop, three free reading-rooms, and four summer resorts. Gifts and legacies have for many years assured it an annual income of nearly two hundred thousand dollars, for its founder did almost as much for the rich as he did for the poor by guiding them to investments which pay dividends in something better than gold. He once happily described the Children's Aid Society as "a connecting link between the fortunate and the unfortunate," and a great multitude hold him in grateful remembrance for forging it.

When stage-coaches still travelled the Boston Road the district lying between Second and Fourth Avenues and Twenty-third and Twenty-seventh Streets was known as Bull's Head Village, and here for many years was the great cattle-market of the city. It was afterwards removed to Forty-second Street, thence to Ninety-fourth Street, and still later to the Jersey shore. A few blocks to the north of the vanished village one comes upon the site of the first house built upon the eastern side of the island north of the Bowery. Hereabouts the East River shore recedes so as to form a considerable indentation, and on the shores of this bay in 1653 lay the many-acred farm of Jacobus Kip, then secretary of the province. In 1654 he took to wife beautiful Marie La Montagne, the belle of New Amsterdam, and the same year reared a house on his farm and went there to live with his bride. Kip's house, a large double structure with an ample wing, was built of bricks brought from Holland, and so well did its builders do their work that it was still in excellent condition when in 1851 it was demolished to make way for long rows of tenement houses and the streets of the City Plan. Second Avenue and Thirty-fifth Street now cross over its site, and give no sign of its existence. The name of its first owner, however, survives in that of the little cove it faced, and which for two centuries and a half has been known as Kip's Bay, though should the worthy Jacobus come alive again he would find it filled with ships and shipping and the green banks where he often fished buried beneath a sprawling ferry-house.

XII

Post-Road & Riverside

THE long-time residence of Peter Cooper, an unpretending yet substantial structure, in keeping with the taste and character of its builder, still stands at the southwest corner of Fourth Avenue and Twenty-eighth Street, and a block away, at No. 123 Lexington Avenue, one finds a modest brownstone house which for many years was the home of Chester A. Arthur. It was there on the night of September 19, 1881, that he received the message that Garfield had ceased to live; in the dimly lighted parlor he took the oath of office as President, and to this house, at a later time, he returned to die.

What was known in the old days as the Middle Road diverged from the Boston Road near the Cooper homestead. Thence it passed to the line of Lexington Avenue, which it followed to what is now Forty-second Street, when it curved to the present Fifth Avenue and ran northward to rejoin the Boston Road at Ninetieth Street. Murray Hill, which it climbed on the way, preserves the name of the Quaker merchant, Robert Murray, whose country-house, set in a wide lawn and bordered on either side by extensive gardens, fronted the road near the present intersection of Fourth Avenue and Thirty-sixth Street. The worthy Quaker called his estate Belmont, and chroniclers of the later colonial period describe it as one of the loveliest spots on the island. It overlooked Kip's Bay, where the British landed when they took possession of the city on September 16, 1776, and it played a memorable part in the events of that memorable day.

It was in a cornfield belonging to the Murray estate, on the site of the Grand Central Station, that Washington on his four-mile gallop from Bloomingdale met and vainly sought to rally the patriot forces in headlong retreat from Kip's Bay; and it was the quick-witted wife of the owner of Belmont who later in the day induced Howe and his generals to tarry over-long at her dinner-table, thus gaining time for the American forces south of Murray Hill to make their escape and join the main army at Harlem Heights. Mrs. Murray, who died soon after this patriotic feat, was a Miss Lindley of Philadelphia, a famous Quaker belle, and her oldest son was Lindley Murray the grammarian, who spent much of his boyhood at Belmont. Murray Hill has continued from the time of its Quaker owner until the present to be a centre of wealth and fashion. It has had many notable residents in later years, but none better remembered than Admiral David G. Farragut, who, after the Civil War, lived for several years and died in the house numbered 113 East Thirty-sixth Street.

When the City Plan still belonged to the future, Murray Hill and Kip's Bay were encircled by two water-courses. One of these streams had its source in the vicinity of Forty-sixth Street, between Fifth and Sixth Avenues, and ran eastward to a point near Fourth Avenue, where it curved to the south, and skirting Murray Hill, flowed into Kip's Bay at Thirty-sixth Street. The other stream rose near Broadway and Forty-fourth Street, and ran southward to Thirty-fourth Street, where it curved to the east, flowing between Thirty-first and Thirty-second Streets to the line of Third Avenue. Then swinging towards the north, it crossed Second Avenue on the line of Thirty-fourth Street, which it followed to the bay. This stream expanded at Madison Avenue into a little lake called Sunfish Pond, which extended to Fourth Avenue and covered the site of the present car-stables. Sunfish Pond, Mines tells us, was famous for its eels, as well as sunfish and flounders. He adds that the brook which fed it was almost dry in summer, but in times of freshet overflowed its banks and spread from the northern line of the present Madison Square to Murray Hill, more than once compelling those who lived along its lower course to resort to boats as the only means of reaching the avenue.

Yet another stream long since blotted out by the execution of the City Plan took its rise in the lower part of the present Central Park, crossed Fifty-ninth Street between Fifth and Sixth Avenues, and then, turning to the east, again crossed Fifty-ninth Street at Madison Avenue. Curving again at Fourth Avenue, it flowed southeast to Second Avenue and Fifty-first Street, and then south to Forty-eighth Street. There it turned sharply to the east, but at First Avenue swung again to the southeast, finding an outlet at Forty-seventh Street. This stream's crooked course to the East River carried it through the northern part of the sixty-acre farm, lying between the present Forty-first and Forty-eighth Streets, which Sir Edmund Andros granted in 1677 to David Duffore, and that worthy building a grist-mill on its bank, it became known, through popular corruption of his name, as De Voor's Mill Stream. The mill disappeared long ago, leaving no trace behind it, and the brook which turned its wheel now finds an outlet through a sewer which discharges into the East River at Forty-ninth Street.

Deutal or Turtle Bay, a rock-bound cove, indented the eastern edge of the Duffore farm, between Forty-fourth and Forty-sixth Streets. Its high and precipitous banks made it a safe and snug harbor for small vessels, and for that reason it was fortified at the opening of the Revolution and again during the second war with England. Howe found Turtle Bay a convenient landing-place when he crossed from Long Island, and it was also the scene of an earlier and, for the patriots, far more gratifying incident of the struggle for independence,—the capture on a stormy night in 1775 by a chosen band of the Sons of Liberty of a magazine of military stores there assembled by the British authorities. Old men with whom the writer has talked recall the storehouse in which these munitions were deposited as standing in their boyhood upon a grass-grown wharf on the southern side of the bay, but to those who were veterans when the last century was young Turtle Bay was best remembered as a favorite pleasure-resort of the townsfolk, famous for its dinners and suppers and for the large parties that gathered there for feasting and frolic.

Threescore years ago there stood on the Boston Road, at the intersection of Third Avenue and Forty-ninth Street, a tiny hamlet, known as Odellville, which took its name from the keeper of a country-tavern, who there nearly lived out a century. Open fields lay to the west of Odellville in that slow-moving time, but to the east a few scattered houses flecked the river-bank, and one of these, set down at the foot of Forty-ninth Street, was for a time the country home of Horace Greeley. The house occupied by the editor of the *Tribune* was a rambling wooden structure, with ample shrubbery and gardens and abundant shade- and fruit-trees, and it was then accessible, as Greeley tells us, only by a long lane from the Boston Road, while the only regular communication with the town was by an hourly stage on Third Avenue. Margaret Fuller was then a writer for the *Tribune* and a member of the Greeley household, and her letters testify to the delight she found in this suburban retreat, —the wide hall and the piazza, the garden and the trees, the rocks and the gliding sails. "I have never been so well situated," she writes to her brother Eugene in New Orleans. "As to a home, the place where we live is old and dilapidated, but in a situation of great natural loveliness. When there I am perfectly secluded, yet every one I wish to see comes to see me, and I can get to the centre of the city in half an hour. The house is kept in a Castle Rackrent style, but there is all affection for me and desire to make me feel at home; and I do feel so, which could scarcely have been expected from such an arrangement. My room is delightful; how I wish you could sit at its window with me and see the sails glide by! As to the public part, that is entirely satisfactory. I do just as I please, and the editors express themselves perfectly satisfied; and others say my pieces tell to a degree I could not expect. I think, too, I shall do better and better. I am truly interested in the great field which opens before me, and it is pleasant to be sure of a chance at half a hundred thousand readers. Mr. Greeley I like, nay, more, love. He is in his habits a plebeian; in his heart a nobleman. His abilities in his own way are great. He believes in mine to a surprising extent. We are true friends."

The house in which Margaret Fuller spent so

many happy and fruitful days long since went the way of most old houses on the Island of Manhattan. Time has also taken the Beekman mansion, which stood for more than a hundred years just west of First Avenue, between Fifty-first and Fifty-second Streets, in a rectangular area bounded by the river and Turtle Bay, and on the west and south by De Voor's Mill Stream. James Beekman built this house in 1763, a plain but massive structure, with two stories and a basement surrounded by an old-fashioned shingle roof, with windows looking out upon Turtle Bay, and with a lawn that reached down to the Boston Road. No other house in the city was richer in historic associations. During the Revolution it was successively occupied by Howe, Chester, and Carleton; it was the scene of the condemnation of Nathan Hale; and beneath its roof André passed his last night in New York before setting out for West Point on the mission which cost him his life.

Madame Riedesel, wife of the Hessian general who surrendered at Saratoga, occupied the Beekman mansion in 1780, and her journal depicts its charms in glowing colors. Her pen lingers over the beauties of lawn and garden and greenhouse,—the same in which Hale spent his last hours,—and she declares that the interior of the house left nothing for a tenant to desire. "The spacious rooms," we are told, "were adorned with black marble mantles bearing elaborate carvings of scroll and foliage. The fireplaces were ornamented with Dutch tiles, representing Scriptural subjects. Elijah in his chariot of fire was the story of one artist, and others had seized upon the history of the prodigal son and the perils of the apostles to impress a moral on the beholder while they delighted him with an odd exhibition of their art." The Beekman house, in its last days a shabby ruin, was demolished in 1874, but the drawing-room mantel and the Dutch tiles have been preserved by the New York Historical Society.

Two blocks from and a little to the east of the site of the Beekman mansion, hard by the foot of Fifty-third Street, stands a house that is, perhaps, the oldest building on the Island of Manhattan. A perfect specimen of the Dutch architecture of two hundred years ago, this house was known long before the Revolution as the Spring Valley farm-house, and the records have it that it was built either by David Duffore or by one of his descendants. After the Revolution it bore the names of Odell and Arden, and later still was known as the Brevoort house and estate. It is a one-story-and-attic structure, with sloping roof and three dormer windows, a broad porch, clapboarded walls, and cross-beams hewn out of solid oak. The Spring Valley farm-house stood in the old days almost at the water's edge, but made ground now extends to the east of it, and its site has become the centre of a straggling lumber-yard. The tall shot-tower that keeps vigil over it was put up in 1821, and has seen the region thereabouts change from open country to a densely populated quarter of the town.

The old mansion which overlooks the East River from a high terrace at the foot of Sixty-first Street belongs to a more recent period than the Spring Valley farm-house. It was built in 1799 by Colonel William S. Smith, who had married the only daughter of President John Adams. Smith had acquired wealth in trade and designed the house as a present for his wife. Accordingly no expense was spared in the building; but when the walls were up and the roof on, Smith failed, and the house, which has ever since been known as Smith's Folly, passed to Monmouth C. Hart, who completed it and opened it as a road-house. Smith's Folly, which at that time must have formed an important stopping-place, consists of two wings and a connecting hall, and is quaint to an unusual degree. Heavy columns support the second, which is also the main, story, and you enter by a door-way flanked on either side by windows whose tiny panes light a hall-way that might have been modelled from sketches by Pyle and Parsons. Nail-studded chests are scattered about, and in one corner a short-banistered stairway leads up to a roomy hall, where candelabra of antique pattern, spindle-legged chairs and tables, and ancient wares of all sorts, some acquired, some made with the house, contribute to the pleasing consistency of the place.

The old house is especially rich in portraits, and in the hall just mentioned there is hardly a foot of wall space not covered with the original or a copy of some famous work of art. There are several Van Dycks, a genuine Raphael Sanzio, one or two Rembrandts, a Tintoretto, a Rubens, a Murillo, and a Claude Lorraine. The most notable of these is the Raphael,—a head of Christ crowned with thorns. Among those who visited Smith's Folly in its road-house days was Jerimal Towle, who, struck by its quaint architecture, bought it when Hart died and made it his home. It was Towle who gathered the paintings which lend added interest to the place. He bought the house in 1834, and it has ever since remained in the possession of his family. It is now occupied by two of his daughters who seek to carry out their father's wishes in its preservation. Here they dwell, well out of the beaten track, but carrying with them delightful recollections of early times, which add pleasure to the quest of those who search for reminders of old New York.

A short walk from Smith's Folly, across and to the west of the Boston Road, brings one to No. 3 East Sixty-sixth Street, and to the brownstone house which was the last home of General Grant. The house was bought by friends and presented to Mrs. Grant in 1879, soon after their return from Europe. Here occurred the most heroic struggle of the general's life. The failure of the firm of Grant & Ward, in which he was a special partner, left him, in the spring of 1884, with hardly a dollar he could call his own. Soon his health failed, and he was told that his span of life must be a brief one. Then it was that the silent captain, gazing as it were into the open grave, nerved himself for his last battle. He had begun his "Personal Memoirs," upon whose sale he counted for the future fortune of his family, but the monetary value of the book would be greatly depreciated if it should be completed by any hand but his own. This thought gave the stricken man courage to contend with fate and to hold death at bay until he could secure a competence to his loved ones.

Well has it been said by his friend Adam Badeau that "the spectacle of the hero who had earned and worn the highest earthly honors, working amid the miseries of a sick-chamber to glean the gains he knew he could never enjoy,—the fainting warrior propped up to stammer out utterances to sell for the benefit of his children,—is a picture to which history in all her annals can find no parallel." Strength of will sustained him through a work that might fairly have occupied a well man trained to literary effort for several years. Every line was either written by General Grant or dictated by him. And he won in the race with death, completing the last chapter on July 19, 1885. His task accomplished, will and strength alike failed, and on the twenty-third of the same month the end came. But his last battle was a triumphant one, for no book written in America by a single hand has ever returned such a large reward. More sufficing, however, is the thought that the unselfish labor which brought this reward made Grant's last days the greatest of a great career.

Fourscore years ago a traveller on the Boston Road coming to the fifth mile-stone from the City Hall would have espied to the west of that thoroughfare a farm owned by Robert Lenox and covering the area now bounded by Fourth and Fifth Avenues and Sixty-eighth and Seventy-fourth Streets. Lenox was a native of Dundee in Scotland who came first to this country in 1779 as a midshipman in the service of George III. He grew to like America well, and a certain maiden of New York better, and when he returned to England it was only to resign from the royal navy. Then he came back to New York, married the woman of his choice, and embarking in trade made for himself before middle life a leading place among the great merchants of his time. He had faith in the future of the city of his adoption, and at an early period became a large owner of land, not only in the lower part of the town, but also in the sparsely settled upper reaches of the island. One of his purchases in the latter quarter was the farm on the Boston Road, which he bought at a total cost of less than seven thousand dollars.

Lenox bought part of his farm to protect the estate of an old friend, and it was his after-belief that he had paid for it much more than it was worth. When he made his will in 1829 he bequeathed "My Farm at the Five-Mile Stone" to his son James Lenox for life, and after his death to his heirs. "My motive for so leaving this property," he declared, "is a firm persuasion that it may at no distant day be the site of a village; and as it cost me much more than its present worth, from circumstances known to my family, I like to cherish the belief that it may be realized to them. At all events I want the experiment made by keeping the property from being sold." Lenox in a later codicil so modified his will as to bequeath the farm without reserve to his son. "At the same time," he added, "I wish him to understand that my opinion respecting the property is not changed, and though I withdraw all legal restrictions to his making sale of the whole or any part of the same, yet I enforce upon him my advice not to do so."

James Lenox gave heed to this sagacious advice. He sold no part of the farm until 1864, when it had become the most valuable, as it was also the largest, parcel of land held by one person within the city limits. Parts of it sold in the year named represented a total value of six million dollars, and to-day the eighteen city blocks included in the farm are worth as many millions. James Lenox never married, and much of the great wealth that came to him was devoted to charity and good works. He founded the Presbyterian Hospital " for the reception of patients of every creed, nationality, and color," giving it in land and money nearly a million dollars, while the highest and choicest spot on his farm was reserved as a site for the library which bears his name. He bequeathed to this institution the whole of the block between Fifth and Madison Avenues and Seventieth and Seventy-first Streets, the library and art treasures collected during his lifetime, and more than seven hundred thousand dollars in money. And all this came from the farm which it was its owner's daring hope would "at no distant day be the site of a village."

In the time when the friends of Robert Lenox marvelled that so shrewd a man could indulge in so fanciful a dream, the East River shore for many blocks north of Seventy-first Street was covered by a forest known as Jones's Wood. The height called Dead Man's Rock marked the beginning of this wood, a place of delight to pleasure-seekers from the distant town in the opening years of the last century. Mines tells us that "it was the last fastness of the forest primeval that once covered the shores of the East River, and its wildness was almost savage. Tradition made it a favorite resort in the infant days of the colony of pirates who dared the terrors of Hell Gate and came here to land their treasures and hold their revels. The ninety acres which composed it passed through many hands until it came into the possession of the Provoost family in 1742, and here they built and occupied for nearly sixty years. The Provoosts were a remarkable family. Samuel Provoost was an assistant minister of Trinity at the opening of the Revolution. An ardent patriot, his preaching gave offence to the Tories, and he was deprived of his position and sent into retirement, to emerge afterwards as first bishop of New York and president of Columbia College. David Provoost, cousin of the bishop, was quite another character. A soldier in Washington's army, and wounded at the battle of Long Island, he became in after years a noted smuggler, having his chief stronghold at Hallet's Point, and successfully defying the officers of the law to the end of his wild career. The fiery old smuggler was laid to rest at the ripe age of ninety. Long afterwards the boys used to gather beside his grave and tell each other wonderful stories of the unearthly doings of the old man's ghost. Not one of them could have been persuaded by all the ready money in the city to keep a night's vigil under the trees that overhung his lonely resting-place."

The Provoosts, after long occupancy, sold their woodland farm to John Jones, but reserved the use of their family vault, cut in a rocky knoll near the foot of Seventy-first Street, and it lay in melancholy ruin long after the woods which surrounded it had become a favorite resort for picnic-parties. Twoscore years ago the northward growth of the town began to rob Jones's Wood of its goodly proportions, and to-day no vestige of it remains. Gone also is the Kissing Bridge of the old days. Where is now the intersection of Third Avenue and Seventy-seventh Street the Boston Road aforetime crossed a small stream known as the Saw-Kill, and the accurate John Randel, Jr., assures us that the bridge which spanned this stream was known to all the young men and women of his day as the Kissing Bridge. The Kissing Bridge of a yet earlier time stood in that section of the Boston

Road which once was Chatham Street, and it was of the older institution that the Rev. William Burnaby wrote in his diary nearly a century and a half ago: "Just before you enter the town there is a little bridge commonly called 'the Kissing Bridge,' where it is customary, before passing beyond, to salute your companion." The reverend gentleman seems to have conformed to this custom, for he adds that he found it "curious, yet not displeasing."

The stream spanned by the Kissing Bridge of Randel's time had its origin in two rills, one of which rose near Eighth Avenue and Eighty-ninth Street and flowed eastward, through the meadow later converted into the Croton Reservoir, to the line of Sixth Avenue, where it curved southeast and crossed Fourth Avenue near Seventy-sixth Street. The other rose in the vicinity of Ninth Avenue and Eighty-fifth Street, and flowed southward to the present Manhattan Square, where it widened into a pond. Then it turned to the east, and, crossing what is now Central Park, joined its sister rill at Seventy-fifth Street near Third Avenue, whence the stream thus formed flowed east to its outlet near the foot of Seventy-fifth Street. The later history of this stream was a sinister one. The

THE LAST OF KISSING-BRIDGE ON THE OLD BOSTON ROAD,
FIFTIETH STREET AND SECOND AVENUE, 1860

greater part of the district drained by it lay below the level of the city sewers, and it was only by the construction of some thousands of feet of deep drains, apart from sewers, that it was finally freed from malarial disorder.

Sixty years ago there was a road-house hard by the fifth mile-stone on the Boston Road, and north of that point the traveller passed only scattered houses, open fields, and bits of woodland until he came to the village of Yorkville, a straggling hamlet which reached from Eighty-third to Eighty-ninth Street and from Fourth to Second Avenue. Old men who knew Yorkville in their boyhood say that it was never a pretty place, but add that the view towards the East River was superb. The Hell Gate ferry was then at the foot of Eighty-sixth Street, opposite the northern end of Blackwell's Island. It was reached by a road that started from the Boston Road just south of Eighty-third Street, and from this shaded lanes led to the country residences of various men of wealth who were wont to speak of their places as being on Hell Gate. The villa of Commodore Isaac Chauncey was south of Eighty-fifth Street and between Avenues A and B; that of John Jacob Astor on the south side of Eighty-eighth Street, his grounds extending from Avenue A to Avenue B and from Eighty-seventh to Eighty-ninth Street; and that of Archibald Gracie east of Avenue B and north of Eighty-eighth Street.

Washington Irving was from time to time a welcome guest at the summer home of Astor. "For upward of a month past," he writes in September, 1835, "I have been quartered at Hell Gate with Mr. Astor, and I have not had so quiet and delightful a nest since I have been in America. He has a spacious and well-built house, with a lawn in front of it and a garden in the rear. The lawn sweeps down to the water-edge, and full in front of the house is the little strait of Hell Gate, which forms a constantly moving picture. I cannot tell you how sweet and delightful I have found this retreat; pure air, agreeable scenery, profound quiet, and perfect command of my time and self. The consequence is that I have written more since I have been here than I have ever done in the same space of time." February of the following year found Irving still at "Mr. Astor's country retreat opposite Hell Gate, giving my last handling to the Astor work. It is this handling which, like the touching and retouching of a picture, gives the richest effects." The work to which

Irving refers was his "Astoria," which he had taken up at Astor's request, and which as a complete and satisfying picture of wild life on the Pacific still finds admiring readers.

The Astor house was torn down many years ago, but the former home of Archibald Gracie stands in an excellent state of preservation in East River Park at the foot of Eighty-ninth Street, and still looks out as of old upon the whirling waters of Hell Gate. Archibald Gracie filled a large place in the New York of his time. He was long one of the merchant princes of the town, and his fleet of clippers with their red and white signals was known in every sea. He had also the soul of a prince, and Oliver Wolcott said of him that "he was one of the excellent of the earth, actively liberal, intelligent, seeking and rejoicing in occasions to do good." His house beside Hell Gate long since passed into the hands of strangers, but Louis Philippe, John Quincy Adams, Josiah Quincy, Washington Irving, and Tom Moore were guests of its founder, and if ghosts walked now its halls should troop with them in still and starless nights.

XIII

When Harlem was a Village

ALL the world, or at least that goodly portion of it familiar with old New York, knows, that in the eleventh year of Peter Stuyvesant's directorship of the affairs of New Amsterdam that testy worthy gave permission for the founding of a village in the upper part of the Island of Manhattan which he decreed should be called New Harlem; whereby hangs an interesting tale of the day of first things. Then north of a line extending from the present Eighth Avenue and One Hundred and Twelfth Street to the East River at One Hundredth Street broad meadows stretched northward and eastward to the river now called the Harlem. Save for a single hill, known to us as Mount Morris Park, it was a level and treeless region, sure to warm the hearts of wanderers who had lately taken leave of the flats and dunes of their motherland. The Indian called it Muscoota, but the white man when he came gave it the name of the Flats, and as early as 1636 a little band of colonists had claimed it for their own.

These pioneers built their homes on the site of an Indian village, at the foot of the hill which they named Slang Berge, or Snake Hill, and which is now Mount Morris Park, and, growing in numbers from year to year, were in 1658 granted permission by Stuyvesant to form a village, to which, as we have seen, he gave the name of New Harlem. After that they determined to erect a tavern and to build a dam and grist-mill. A site for the mill was found on the banks of the creek, twenty feet deep and a hundred wide, which ran along the southern edge of The Flats, and emptied into Hell Gate Bay, near the foot of One Hundred and Sixth Street. This creek had two branches, one of which rose in the rocks east of Bloomingdale, and ran north and east through McGowan's Pass to the present crossing of Fifth Avenue and One Hundred and Ninth Street. The other and larger branch had its source in a number of springs at the base of the hills which flanked The Hollow Way at the foot of One Hundred and Twenty-fourth Street and flowed eastward to Fifth Avenue and One Hundred and Seventeenth Street, where it swung towards the south to join the southern branch, and then took its way east along the line of One Hundred and Sixth Street.

The men of New Harlem built a dam across this stream in 1667, a little west of the present Third Avenue, and at its northern end a grist-mill. Two bridges were thrown over the stream, one just below the dam and the other, across which the Boston Road ran in after years, west of the present Fifth Avenue. One Derick Benson bought pond and mill in 1730, and both were thenceforth called by his name. The mill was burned during the Revolution, but was rebuilt by Benjamin Benson after the war, and remained in operation until in 1827 work was begun on the Harlem Canal. This canal extended from the East River nearly to Fifth Avenue, following in part the line of Harlem Creek, and was part of an ambitious scheme for a water highway sixty feet wide to be extended through the Hollow Way to the Hudson. Such part of it as came into being was solidly built of stone, but failure overtook the enterprise, and at a later time both canal and creek were filled in to furnish sites for rows of houses.

When this abortive canal was yet a part of the remote future, and the village of New Harlem still nestled about Snake Hill, it received a visit in 1679 from those keen-eyed travellers, the Labadist missionaries Dankers and Sluyter. They tell us in their journal that after leaving the Bowery they proceeded " through the woods to New Harlem, a rather large village directly opposite the place where the northeast creek (Harlem River) and the East River come together, situated about three hours' journey from New Amsterdam, like as the old Harlem in Europe is situated about three hours' distance from the old Amsterdam. As our guide, Gerrit, had some business here, and found many acquaintances, we remained over night at the house of the schout of the village, who had formerly lived in Brazil, and whose heart was still full of it. His house was all the time filled with people, mostly drinking execrable rum. He had also the best cider we have tasted."

The morning after this lively night at the house of Resolved Waldron, constable of New Harlem, the Labadists set out for the northern end of the island. " When we were not far from the point of Spuyten Duyvil," they write, " we could see on our left the rocky cliffs of the main-land on the other side of the North River standing straight up and down with the grain, just as if they were antimony. We crossed over the Spuyten Duyvil in a canoe, and . . . followed the opposite side of the land until we came to the house of one Valentyn. He had gone to the city, but his wife, though she did not know Gerrit or us, was so much rejoiced to see Hollanders that she hardly knew what to do for us. She set before us what she had. We left after breakfasting. Her son showed us the way, and we came to a road entirely covered with peaches. We asked the boy why they left them to lie there, and why the hogs did not eat them. He answered, 'We do not know what to do with them, there are so many; the hogs are satiated with them and will not eat any more.' . . . We pursued our way now a small distance through the woods and over the hills, then back again along the shore to a point where lived an Englishman named Webblingh, who was standing ready to cross over. He carried us over with him, and refused to take any pay for our passage, offering us at the same time some of his rum, a liquor which is everywhere. We were now again at New Harlem, and dined with Resolved, at whose house we had slept the night before, and who made us welcome."

Save for the Indian wars of Kieft's time, for the better part of two hundred years the ways of

New Harlem were slow-going and peaceful ones. An early task of the settlers was to build a church, and as soon as they were able they replaced the original structure with one of stone, which boasted an arched door, a steeple, and a weather-cock. The church which stood until 1825 at One Hundred and Twenty-fifth Street, midway between Second and Third Avenues, faced an old Indian trail leading to the Harlem River, and this trail became Harlem Road or Church Lane, the main thoroughfare of the village. A line drawn from the northeastern corner of One Hundred and Nineteenth Street and Lexington Avenue to the same corner of One Hundred and Twenty-third Street and Second Avenue, and thence to the river, would pass through the centre of Church Lane. The tavern on Church Lane became in 1673 the first halting-place of the monthly mail established between New York and Boston by way of Harlem, but it was not until a century later that the eastern post-road was opened, and mail-coaches went through once a week, pausing for refreshment at Harlem.

Nor at first did the Boston Road follow its present course across and beyond the Harlem River. Instead it joined the Kingsbridge Road near One Hundred and Thirty-first Street, and following it northwest to Spuyten Duyvil so passed off the Island of Manhattan. At a later time, however, a ferry was established at the foot of Church Lane, where One Hundred and Twenty-sixth Street touches the Harlem River, and by this new and shorter route the Boston Road thereafter took its way to the north. The ferry-house at the foot of Church Lane remained standing for many years, and when demolished in 1867 it was, with one exception, the last relic of the ancient village of New Harlem.

Beyond the Harlem River in the old days lay the wide-spreading lands of the Morris family, near its mouth the home of Gouverneur Morris, and close at hand the country-seat of his brother Lewis Morris, one of the signers of the Declaration of Independence. Richard Morris, first of his line in America, was an officer in Cromwell's army, who fled from England after the Restoration, and purchased north of the Harlem a manor ten miles square, to which he gave the name of Morrisania. Richard's son Lewis became chief justice of the province, and from him in the third generation descended Gouverneur Morris, who was one of the ablest of the builders of the republic, and something more,—wit,

"VIEW OF HARLAEM FROM MORISANIA, IN THE PROVINCE OF NEW YORK, SEPTEMBER, 1765"

philosopher, and successful manager of large affairs. A graduate of King's College and early admitted to the bar, Gouverneur Morris served during the Revolution in the Provincial Congress of New York and in the Continental Congress, taking a leading part in the deliberations of both bodies. Afterwards he was a delegate to the constitutional convention, and no man did better work in the great task of forming the Constitution, the first draft of which came from his hand.

Private business took Morris to France in 1789, and the next nine years of his life were spent in Europe. He was in Paris during the Revolution, part of the time serving as American minister, and his diary furnishes one of the most vivid and sufficing accounts of those dark times that have come down to us. He returned to America in 1799, and was chosen almost at once to fill an unexpired term in the Federal Senate. His brief period of service in that body ended in 1803, but he continued to the end to play a prominent part in public affairs, and was a leader in starting the project of the Erie Canal. He spent his last years at Morrisania, tilling his farm, receiving visits from his friends, and carrying on a wide correspondence on business and politics. He married in 1809 most happily, and a letter sent not long afterwards to an old friend in France gives us a delightful glimpse of himself and his home life. "My health," he writes, "is excellent, saving a little of the gout which at this moment annoys me. I can walk three leagues, if the weather be pleasant and the road not rough. My employment is to labor for myself a little, for others more; to receive much company and forget half those who come. I think of public affairs a little, play a little, read a little, and sleep a good deal. With good air, a good cook, fine water and wine, a good constitution, and a clear conscience I descend towards the grave full of gratitude to the Giver of all good."

Morris died after a brief illness in 1816, and was buried beneath the church his family had erected on their lands,—St. Ann's Church, Morrisania. His estate descended to his only son, and from the latter a large part of it passed into the hands of strangers to spring into vigorous life as the village of Morrisania. The elder Jordan L. Mott purchased some hundreds of acres of the Morris lands, and established thereon an iron-foundry and a town, to which he gave the name of Mott Haven, and which, like Morrisania, has now become an integral part of the city. The growing town going still farther afield has also claimed the village of West Farms, where of old the De Lanceys had their country-seat, and strove with the Morrises for supremacy in local affairs. It was at West Farms in the opening days of the Revolution that Aaron Burr led an assault on a block-house built by Oliver De Lancey, the boldness and rapidity of the manœuvre causing the Tory garrison to surrender without a shot in its defence.

Harlem also contributed more than one stirring incident to the history of the struggle for independence. Among the early settlers in the village were the McGowns (written in history as McGowan), who built their home and gave a name to the rocky pass still traceable in the upper part of Central Park. When, after the repulse of the British at the battle of Harlem Heights, Howe moved up his entire army from the city to retrieve the disaster, his advance guard, a Hessian brigade, halted at the McGown homestead, and found that the only male person at home was a lad of twelve, Andrew McGown, whose father was in Washington's army. The boy was pressed into service to guide the column against the American camp. He obeyed with apparent willingness, but led the Hessians by a roundabout course to the shores of the Hudson while the patriot forces were taking themselves out of the way and camping behind their intrenchments at Fort Washington. Mines, in relating the incident, has well said that a boy that day was the salvation of his country.

For so long a while did Harlem remain a secluded hamlet tucked away at the northern end of the island that as late as 1830 the only passenger conveyance between the village and New York was by a stage, which left the corner of Third Avenue and One Hundred and Twenty-fifth Street at seven in the morning and reached Park Row shortly before ten o'clock, starting on the return trip at three in the afternoon. A few years later the stages began making hourly trips, but a visitor describes the village in the fifties as still "clustered close to the river, well shaded with trees, most charmingly rural, and apparently impervious to change." Though the New York and Harlem Railway Company was incorporated in 1831, it was not until 1840 that the first steam-train was put in operation between Thirty-second and One Hundred and Twenty-fifth Streets. Twenty-five years later the horse-cars had come into being, but it took them nearly an hour and a half to convey passengers from One Hundred and Twenty-ninth Street to City

Hall; and it was not until the completion of the elevated roads in 1880 that Harlem entered fairly upon the career that in a little more than twenty years has made it the abiding-place of a million people. Now solid blocks of apartment-houses, stretching mile upon mile, cover The Flats of the old days, and Harlem has lost all semblance of its earlier self.

Besides the Boston Road, one other thoroughfare connected New York with Harlem when the last century was young. This was the Bloomingdale Road, which, starting from the present Union Square, followed the line of Broadway and the Boulevard through the village from which it took its name, skirted the foot of the hill where Manhattanville afterwards nestled, and joined the Kingsbridge Road near the present crossing of One Hundred and Forty-seventh Street and Ninth Avenue. The Boulevard has blotted out the middle and upper reaches of the Bloomingdale Road, filling its valleys, levelling its hillocks, and straightening its crooks and turns, but Dayton tells us that in his boyhood it was still "a country drive of unsurpassed beauty, up hill and down dale, varied with many a curve, and at short intervals enlivened by an enchanting view of the Hudson."

The road was laid out before 1707, and wealthy citizens early chose the region through which it ran as sites for their country-seats. One of these was Oliver De Lancey, whose roomy house faced the road near the present Seventieth Street. De Lancey ranged himself against his countrymen when the Revolution came, and in 1777 the patriots put an end to his home on the Bloomingdale Road. It was on a cold night in November of that year, the gloomiest of the long struggle, that a party of Americans descended the Hudson intent upon retaliating in some way for the atrocities perpetrated by the British in their forays through the neighboring country. After a hard battle with the ice that filled the river they managed to anchor their boat near the Bloomingdale landing. The women of the family and the servants were the only occupants of the De Lancey homestead. The soldiers, after reconnoitring, applied the torch to the building and burned it to the ground. Mrs. De Lancey found shelter in a stone outhouse, while Charlotte De Lancey and Elizabeth Floyd, two young girls of sixteen, escaped shoeless and hatless to a near-by swamp, where they concealed themselves until morning, when they were discovered by neighbors. The house was never rebuilt, and its site until a recent period was occupied by a small grove of trees.

Fate has dealt more kindly with the old stone house yet standing at West End Avenue and Seventy-ninth Street, which was built about 1759 by one Van Der Huevel, then governor of Demerara. Yellow fever was raging in the South American colony at the time, and it was Van Der Huevel's intention to return to his post when it had spent its force, but, charmed with New York, he concluded to make it his home, and, buying property, built the mansion which bears his name. The house was two stories high, with a steep gable roof and walls of solid stone. The main floor had an arched central hall, with a drawing-room at one side and at the other a lofty dining-room. The upper floor had four large rooms, and over these, in the gable, were the sleeping-apartments. Half a century ago fire destroyed the third or gable roof, and when it was rebuilt it was carried straight up, so that now the house has two stories of stone and one of wood. The house with its four hundred acres was abandoned by the Van Der Huevels during the Revolution, and at a later time became a road-house under the name of Burnham's Mansion House. After that it was bought by a Frenchman named Poillon, who in 1878 sold it to the Astor estate. It has been occupied since 1880 by a florist, whose greenhouses cover a large part of the block, but will no doubt soon go the way of most old houses in New York.

Five years after Van Der Huevel took up his residence on the Bloomingdale Road, Charles Ward Apthorpe, a leading lawyer of the city, bought a two-hundred-acre farm in the same region, and in its centre built a mansion which gave impressive evidence of its owner's wealth. The Apthorpe house stood between the present Ninetieth and Ninety-first Streets and Columbus and Amsterdam Avenues, and was approached by a lane that extended from the Bloomingdale Road to Harlem Commons, between Ninety-third and Ninety-fourth Streets. Its recessed portico was supported by Corinthian columns, and a high arched door-way opened into a hall extending from front to rear and wide enough for a cotillon party, while the great rooms above and below had walls, mantel-pieces, and ceilings of English oak. Outside an ample lawn, dotted with groves of elm-, locust-, and cherry-trees, stretched down towards the Hudson.

Washington had his head-quarters at the Apthorpe house when the British army crossed from

Long Island in September, 1776, and remained there until Silliman's brigade, which was supposed to be hemmed in by the enemy, was led to safety by Aaron Burr. The same evening Howe and his staff occupied the mansion, and there the British commander had his head-quarters and nursed his wounded honor after the battle of Harlem Heights. Indeed, it was whispered about that he was made very welcome there, and that Apthorpe was a royalist at heart. Apthorpe's name at the war's end was included in the list of those suspected of being Tory sympathizers, and he had to suffer the confiscation of the large estates owned by him in Maine and Massachusetts. His New York property, however, was untouched, and he continued to reside in Bloomingdale until his death. That event befell in 1797, but through the first half of the last century the mansion he had builded remained a centre of social triumphs. Then it was converted into a public house in what was known as Elm or Wendell Park, and in 1892 was torn down to make way for a row of apartment-houses. The church, clergy-house, choir, and school-rooms of St. Agnes's Chapel stand upon a portion of the old Apthorpe ground.

When the Apthorpe mansion still fronted the

Bloomingdale Road, a few blocks to the south of it a steep lane led to a secluded nook by the river-side called Stryker's Bay, where was a modest road-house conducted by Joseph Francis, whom men remember as the inventor of the life-boat. A native of Boston and born with his century, Francis while a growing lad resolved to devote his life to the improvement of appliances for rescue at sea. He made his first model of a life-boat when he was twelve years old, kept up his experiments, and at last, in 1845, when landlord of the road-house at Stryker's Bay, was able to patent a boat built of corrugated iron which he was confident could do the work for which it was intended. Then he tried to induce the government to introduce it into general use, but the Secretary of the Treasury declared that there never had been nor ever could be a boat built that would carry people off a wreck. The Secretary said, however, that if Francis had a mind to take his boat down on the Jersey coast and wait until a wreck came along to try it on, the government would like to know the result. If it did half he said it would, then the government would look into it.

Francis was willing to take the chance. He sent his boat to the Jersey coast, hired a crew of hardy coastmen to man it, and drilled them carefully in its use. Soon the British ship "Ayrshire" came driving ashore in a furious storm. It was fast breaking to pieces and its passengers and crew, two hundred souls in all, seemed doomed to death, when Francis's life-boat came to the rescue. Forty times it went to and fro between the stranded ship and the shore, and by it all on board were rescued save one, and he perished through no fault of boat or crew. This splendid feat made Francis the hero of the day. When he went abroad the same year, Napoleon knighted him and gave him a gold snuff-box, the Emperor of Austria and the Czar of Russia heaped honors and decorations upon him, and a dozen other kings and potentates followed their example, hailing him as a benefactor of humanity. Official recognition of his services by his own country did not come until a later time; but when he was ninety, and had earned the title of Father of the Life-saving Service in America, Congress bestowed upon him a gold medal in commemoration of an unexampled career. Content with a moderate fortune, Francis passed his last days in peace and honor, dying in 1893 at the age of ninety-three.

Talleyrand was once a dweller on the Bloomingdale Road, and so was Louis Philippe, though the tradition that the latter taught school there is a misleading one. The future king and his two brothers travelled in America between 1796 and 1798, and during their stay in New York lodged for a time with the Somerindyke family in Bloomingdale. American visitors at Versailles in after years found the Citizen King ever eager to recall and describe in detail what he had seen of their country, but regarding one feature of his memorable journey he always maintained a discreet silence. It was Gouverneur Morris who gave Louis Philippe money wherewith to voyage to America, also furnishing him with unlimited credit during his wanderings in the United States. The bourgeois king's after-treatment of this loan showed the meanest and smallest side of his bourgeois character. "When he came into his own again," writes Morris's biographer, "he at first appeared to forget his debt entirely, and when his memory was jogged, he merely sent Morris the original sum without a word of thanks; whereupon Morris, rather nettled, and as prompt to stand up for his rights against a man in prosperity as he had been to help him when in adversity, put the matter in the hands of his lawyer, through whom he notified Louis Philippe that if the affair was to be treated on a merely business basis it should then be treated in a strictly business way, and the interest for the twenty years that had gone by should be forwarded also. This was done, although not until after the death of Morris, the sum refunded being seventy thousand francs."

Memories of Joseph Bonaparte also cling to the Bloomingdale Road. The ex-king of Spain sought a refuge in America soon after the close of the second war with England, and during his first weeks in New York was an inmate of what was then the country-seat of the Post family, but is now the Claremont, near the Bloomingdale Road at One Hundred and Twenty-third Street. A story is related of him while here that shows that his was the mind of a philosopher. Walking early one morning near the river's edge, his attention was attracted by several squirrels leaping and jumping from the branches of the trees on the hill-side. He watched them as they became more daring in their play and made longer leaps each time. Suddenly the largest one, after a rough-and-tumble contest with its companion, darted at full speed along a limb, leaped for a neighboring tree, missed it, and fell heavily to the ground. "Such is life," observed the ex-king. " By small successes we are led on to greater efforts, until finally——" At this moment the foot of the speaker came in contact with the spongy ground bordering a small ditch, and before he could finish his sage remark he found himself in three feet of muddy water. He picked himself up, however, without much trouble, and upon his return to Claremont directed his servant to go down to the river near the bend, and where he found the footprints of a man deeply embedded in the mud to cut a notch in the nearest tree as a reminder of the second downfall of the brother of Napoleon.

Joseph Bonaparte's stay in America had a sequel not set down in the history-books. Before leaving Europe he had become the owner of a large tract of land in Jefferson county, New York, and in 1822 he settled upon this wilderness estate, installing as mistress of the villa which he built there the daughter of a Philadelphia family, Annette Savage, of whom he always spoke as " the beautiful Quaker girl." When the ex-king returned to Europe in 1830, his " American wife" and the daughter who had been born to them remained in Northern New York. Forty years later this daughter and her husband, Benton by name, found their way to

Paris, where friends laid before the emperor her right to recognition as a Bonaparte. Napoleon III. made an appointment to receive her at the Tuileries, and immediately upon seeing her said, " I recognize you as a Napoleon." A decree was forthwith recorded legitimizing the union of Joseph Bonaparte and Annette Savage, and Mrs. Benton was received as the first cousin of the emperor. Following the downfall of Napoleon III., she returned to America, and after supporting herself by teaching music in Watertown and Utica, finally died in humble lodgings at Richfield Springs. She was laid to rest on a stormy day in December, 1891, in the cemetery of the Presbyterian Church, at Oxbow, New York, only four persons standing beside the grave of this daughter of a king.

Such are the memories, grave and gay, called to mind by a stroll along the Bloomingdale Road. Now its westward reaches have become Riverside Park, perhaps the most beautiful of the city's pleasure-grounds, and on the heights of Claremont rises the tomb of General Grant. More fitting sepulchre could not have been found for the man who has taken his place in history among the world's leaders who live forever more.

XIV

The Way to the Neutral Ground

ONLY the ghosts of coaches long since crumbled into dust now travel the Kingsbridge Road, but it runs as of old from Harlem to the Neutral Ground, and beside it, as in an earlier time, stands the home to which Roger Morris took his bride, and which, with a single exception, has had a more varied and interesting history than any other to be met with on the Island of Manhattan. Frederick Philipse, second lord of Philipse Manor, had a charming daughter, Mary by name, who, tradition has it, declined the hand of George Washington, then a colonel of militia and a rising man of his province, in order to become the wife of Roger Morris, aide-de-camp to Braddock and Washington's comrade-in-arms in the disastrous fight in which the British general lost his life. They were married in January, 1758, and the bride's dowry in her own right was a large domain, plate, jewelry, and money, while she received as a present from her brother, third and last lord of the manor, the house now bounded by Edgecombe Road and Jumel Terrace and One Hundred and Sixtieth and One Hundred and Sixty-second Streets. Here Colonel Morris and his wife lived until the Revolution. Then the husband, having worn the king's uniform, held it a point of honor to preserve a condition of neutrality, and this compelled his flight to England.

The Morris mansion was seized by the Continental troops, and in the summer of 1776 Washington made his head-quarters in the home of his successful rival for a fair woman's hand. The apartment occupied by him as a sleeping-room is shown to visitors, so also are the room at the end of the great hall used as a council-chamber by the general and his staff, and the tree on the lawn to which the former was accustomed to tie his horse. Compelled to face an army of veterans which outnumbered his band of raw recruits two to one, Washington in the autumn of 1776 retreated across the Harlem and encamped near White Plains. It was after this retreat that the Morris mansion played its part in one of the most exciting incidents of his military career. On the heights, a mile to the north of the mansion, the patriots at the opening of the war had built a fort with strong outworks, called Fort Washington. When the retreat into Westchester was ordered, twelve hundred men were left behind to garrison the fort, but were soon besieged in force by the British and their Hessian and Tory allies. From Fort Lee, on the farther shore of the Hudson, Washington anxiously watched their advance, fearful as to the outcome.

When word came to him that a demand had been made for a surrender, he crossed the river with Generals Putnam, Greene, and Mercer, and cautiously made his way to the Morris mansion. From an upper room of the house he was making a hurried survey of the condition of affairs at the fort when the wife of a Pennsylvania soldier, who had come with her husband to the field, and who on the present occasion had followed the chief from the river, stole to his side and whispered something in his ear. Instantly Washington ordered his companions into the saddle, and they galloped post-haste back to the boats that had brought them from the Jersey shore. Fifteen minutes after their flight a British regiment, which had been quietly climbing the heights, appeared in front of the house. A woman's quick eye had been the first to discover its approach, and her timely warning had saved Washington from capture, thus averting a heavy, perhaps a fatal blow to the patriot cause.

Roger Morris returned to New York when peace was concluded, but only to share the fate of the avowed royalists. His own and his wife's property was confiscated, and, again quitting America, he died soon after in England, his friends said of a broken heart. His widow survived him more than thirty years, rearing a family, one of whom became an admiral in the English navy. His son, in turn, was one of the most learned of English naturalists. The title to the house beside the Kingsbridge Road remained in dispute until 1810, when John Jacob Astor bought up the claim of the Morris heirs. Astor a little later sold the house to Stephen Jumel, and thus it entered upon another brilliant period of its history. Jumel was a Frenchman who after an adventurous youth had settled in New York, and, prospering in trade, had become one of the leading merchants of the town. When his fortune was secured he courted and won a beautiful New England girl, and purchased the Morris mansion as a home for his bride. The old house was refitted with hangings, plate, and furniture brought from France, madame's drawing-room being furnished with chairs and divans that had been the property of Marie Antoinette. The Jumels dispensed a generous hospitality, and their New-Year's feasts were counted among the memorable social events of the period. Jerome Bonaparte, he who married and deserted high-spirited Betty Patterson, was a frequent guest at their home, and when they visited Paris, after the death of Napoleon, they were received in the most exclusive salons. A portrait of madame painted during this trip shows a beautiful matron, clad in a robe of blue velvet, with collars and lappets of lace.

Jumel died in 1832, and a year later his widow was courted by Aaron Burr, then almost an octogenarian, but still retaining in generous measure the powers of fascination that in an earlier time had given him so much success with women. Burr was poor and under a cloud; madame was rich and unwilling to wed again; but he pushed his suit with an ardor that brooked no refusal, and finally, after repeated rebuffs, told her that on a certain day he should come with a clergyman, and she must then yield to his importunities. He kept his word; and one sunny afternoon in July, riding up to the great portico, accompanied by the minister who half a century before had married him to the mother of his daughter Theodosia, he insisted that Madame Jumel should then and there become his wife. Alarmed and dismayed, but fearing a scandal, she reluctantly consented, and they were married in the drawing-room of the mansion. A few days later, in this same room,—so the gossips told the story,—madame discovered Burr in the act of kissing a pretty serving-maid, and, boxing his ears, ordered him from the house. Be this as it may, Parton, than whom we could have no better authority, says that Burr rapidly squandered his wife's wealth, and when she demanded an accounting coolly informed her that it was none of her affairs and that her husband could manage her estate. Quite naturally there were bitter quarrels between the ill-matched couple, followed by tardy reconciliations, and at last, in 1834, a permanent separation.

Madame survived this separation thirty-one years, her last days contrasting strangely with her youth and middle life. Wilful always, her eccentricities became more manifest as age crept upon her. Towards the end she lived like a recluse and miser, seeing few visitors and hoarding the fruits of her estate in an unused chamber, and her death was a sad and lonely one.

Her former home, with the plot upon which it stands, is about to become the property of the city. Strongly built, it is in an excellent state of preservation, promising to outlive the century, and nowhere can a more delightful hour be spent than in wandering about its rooms and the surrounding grounds. Washington's old council-chamber has been in some ways altered, but the drawing-room in which madame and Burr were married and the room on the second floor in which the former died, are unchanged, and no "modern improvements" mar the solid, antique exterior of the house, which reminds one of an aged aristocrat standing proudly silent amid the clamor of struggling nobodies.

It was while Washington occupied the Morris mansion that he had his attention called to Alexander Hamilton, then a young captain of artillery, and there began the friendship so big with results for their country. A mile from the Morris mansion Hamilton, when his public career was ended, selected the site for his home. Hamilton Grange, however, no longer occupies its original site. It stood until a few years ago at the corner of Tenth Avenue and One Hundred and Forty-second Street, but now adjoins St. Luke's Protestant Episcopal Church, of which it is the parish school. When bought by Hamilton it included the plot extending from St. Nicholas to Tenth Avenue and from One Hundred and Forty-first to One Hundred and Forty-fifth Street. It was then eight miles from the centre of the city, and Hamilton chose it mainly for its quiet and seclusion. Here, when the house was finished in 1802, he brought his wife and children, and here, no doubt, for he was then but forty-five and in the prime of his powers, he hoped to pass many happy and honored years. Sad and sudden was the ending of this pleasant dream. On the morning of July 11, 1804, he rode forth to face the pistol of an adversary, and in the wooded glade at Weehawken Burr's bullet laid him low. A few hours later friends brought him, desperately wounded, to a house in Greenwich Village, where he died the following day. He is buried, as we know, in Trinity church-yard.

Hamilton Grange is a square, two-storied structure, with a basement, built of wood, and painted a dull brown. There are verandas for the first floor on the east and west sides, and a long flight of steps runs down sidewise from a rear porch. The main entrance is also fronted by a porch, where Mrs. Hamilton, the daughter of Philip Schuyler, used to wait for her husband, when, on warm summer afternoons he came galloping up the Kingsbridge Road from his office in the distant town, and perhaps watched the growth of the thirteen trees Hamilton had planted in honor of the thirteen original States. These trees are still standing, a little removed from the first site of the house, while other trees stud the lawn, and a ragged border of box, showing the growth of years, runs along the abandoned carriage-drive. The front door of the house opens into a small hall-way, and to the right is a spacious room used by Hamilton as a library and study. Adjoining it, also on the right, is the dining-room, low-studded, octagonal in shape, and having a bay-window at the east. Woodwork, mantel, and fireplace are severe in irony of human hopes and ambitions.

From Hamilton Grange a leisurely half-hour's walk, past Trinity Cemetery, opened in 1843 and the last resting-place of many famous Americans, brings one to Audubon Park, which fronts the Hudson between One Hundred and Fifty-fifth and One Hundred and Fifty-eighth Streets. Audubon, the ornithologist, bought the property in 1841, after an adventurous career that had led him over half the

TREES PLANTED BY ALEXANDER HAMILTON AT ONE HUNDRED AND FORTY-THIRD STREET, EAST OF AMSTERDAM AVENUE

world. It consisted of forty-four acres, all heavily wooded, and at that time was almost as remote from the city as a lodge in the Catskills. Here he built a house, his nearest neighbor being Madame Jumel. The naturalist took with him a colony of workmen, carpenters, smiths, and masons, and houses were built in the woods for their shelter while the larger structure went up. Sixty years ago the journey to New York was by no means an easy one, and Audubon raised his own vegetables, and at one time killed his own meat. The Audubon house was the scene of the final triumph of the inventor of the telegraph. When Morse, in 1843, was setting up his first line of telegraph between Philadelphia and New York, its New Jersey terminus was at Fort Lee, opposite Audubon Park. The wire was ferried across the river in a row-boat and the instrument set up in the laundry of the mansion. From this old room, in which there has been no change in half a century, the first telegraph message sent from New York was flashed across the wire, recording the success of the experiment. It was sent in the presence of Morse, Audubon, and the latter's family.

Between 1843 and 1845 Audubon was absent in the West. Soon after his return from this trip his health gave way, he being afflicted with loss of memory. He spent hours in endeavoring to paint, and would burst into tears to find that his efforts were in vain. He had broken his right arm in his youth by a fall from a horse, and had taught himself to paint equally well with either hand, but now both lost their cunning. In 1847 his bedchamber was moved down-stairs, adjoining his old painting-room, and there he died in February, 1851. The old house has been much changed since it passed in 1864 from the possession of the Audubon family. A mansard-roof has been added and bow-windows extended from the front and rear sides. The basement and the first floor, however, have been little altered since the house was built, and standing as it does well out of the beaten track, it serves to add zest to the quest of any searcher after brick-and-mortar reminders of old New York.

Another mile to the north, with a turn to the west from the Kingsbridge Road at One Hundred and Eighty-first Street, brings one to the site of Fort Washington, rich in heroic memories of the birth-year of the republic. It was in the opening days of November, 1776, that General Howe, foiled in his attack upon Washington, then encamped near White Plains, resolved upon the capture of this fort, built by the patriots to guard the entrance to the Hudson. Accordingly he came down from White Plains to the junction of the Harlem and Hudson, while Knyphausen, with his Hessians, advanced to Kingsbridge, and Lord Percy occupied the level ground to the south and east of the fort, thus surrounding it on all but the river-side. Colonel Robert Magaw, commandant of the fort, had only twelve hundred men with which to defend it, and he had also to contend with treachery in his own ranks. William Demont, Magaw's adjutant-general, on the night of November 2, stole away in the darkness to the camp of Lord Percy, carrying plans of the fort, with complete information as to the works and garrison. Thus assured that he could capture the fortress without loss, Howe, on November 15, summoned Magaw to surrender under penalty of a storm, and gave him two hours to decide. "I will not surrender. Take the fort if you can," was the answer of Magaw.

A few hours later the British began their attack, and a heavy artillery fire was in progress, when eighteen hundred soldiers, with Generals Greene and Putnam crossed from Fort Lee, and came to the aid of their comrades. Meanwhile, Washington, advised of the impending attack, had hurried down from Hackensack, where he was arranging for the reception of his army, then crossing the Hudson at Peekskill, and from Fort Lee anxiously watched the assault of the enemy. All day long the cannonading continued, until the white powder fog hid the tree-tops. When night fell Washington embarked in a row-boat to cross the river and find out the true state of affairs, but midway between the two shores met Greene and Putnam, who told him that with the reinforcements which had arrived Magaw could withstand the odds pitted against him. Thus reassured, and little dreaming that it was treason with which Magaw must contend, Washington with Greene and Putnam returned to Fort Lee to await the issue of the morrow's fight. Washington, it should be added, had been in favor of abandoning the fort after the battle of White Plains, but governed by an order from Congress that it should not be given up save under direst extremity, he had left its evacuation to the discretion of Greene, who was on the spot and confident that the garrison could be withdrawn to the Jersey shore if matters came to the worst.

Early on the morning of November 16 Magaw made careful preparation for the desperate work before him. The high ground west of the Harlem River, between what is now One Hundred and Ninety-second and One Hundred and Ninety-sixth Streets (afterwards fortified by the British and named Fort George), was occupied by Colonel Baxter with his Maryland riflemen. Another detachment under Rawlins was posted to the east of the fort, while Cadwallader's regiment of the Pennsylvania Line took its station to the south, in the direction of New York. Hardly were these preparations completed when the British, who knew precisely the strength they were to overcome, began their attack. Down from Kingsbridge came Knyphausen with five hundred Hessians and Waldeckers; and from Harlem Flats Percy, accompanied by Howe, came charging up with a British column; while Matthews, supported by Cornwallis, landed on the Harlem River, where now is the foot of Two Hundredth Street, and advanced towards the fort under cover of the guns on the Westchester hills.

The fierce yet hopeless fight that followed came soon to an end. Knyphausen fell upon Rawlins, and forced him to retreat under cover of the guns of the fort, while Percy, crossing the Harlem with eight hundred men, drove in the American pickets and attacked Cadwallader.

Here the odds were four to one, but so stubborn was the resistance of the Pennsylvanians, that Percy was finally compelled to draw off and to find refuge for the moment behind a near-by strip of woods. Elsewhere the British swept all before them. Matthews, pushing up the wooded heights, drove Baxter from Fort George. Stirling, with a part of Cornwallis's force, descended the Harlem, landed within the American lines at what is now the intersection of Eighth Avenue and One Hundred and Fifty-second Street, and advanced upon Cadwallader, who was retreating along the Hudson pursued by his late opponents. The Pennsylvanians, caught between two fires, again proved their resolute bravery; but they were now outnumbered twenty to one and compelled to surrender. Then it was that Washington, with Greene and Putnam, crossed from Fort Lee, and ascended the heights to the Morris mansion. A quick survey of the field from an upper window told him that the fort was lost, and hardly, as we have seen, had he left the house to recross the river, before Stirling rushed up with his troops and took possession of it.

It had the while become clear to Magaw that to longer hold the works now crowded with the troops driven in from the outer batteries meant futile sacrifice of life. He accordingly signed articles of capitulation, and a little after one o'clock in the afternoon the British flag went up over Fort Washington. The capture cost the British nearly five hundred men in killed and wounded. The Americans lost less than one hundred and fifty, but two thousand eight hundred were captured, many of them to die in the prison-pens of the city. After the surrender some of the Hessians, maddened by the stubborn resistance they had encountered, began murdering their prisoners in cold blood. We are told that from Fort Lee Washington witnessed the fall of the fort " with his usual iron composure, but when he saw his brave men thrown down and stabbed to death, his over-wrought heart could bear it no longer, and he cried and sobbed like a child." Fortunately, British officers hastened to rebuke the Hessians and to stay their slaughter of the helpless.

Visitors to the site of Fort Washington find its ramparts still sharply defined, and are able with little difficulty to trace the outlying redoubts. The ground is covered with trees, and under many of them are little stone tablets which testify to the bravery of the men who there died for their country. The last survivor of the battle of Fort Washington was John Battin, an Englishman, who died in this city in 1852 at the age of one hundred and four years. He remained in America after the Revolution, and for many years kept a public house at the corner of John and Nassau Streets.

Beyond Fort George, now a resort for pleasure-seekers, the Kingsbridge Road takes its way across a long stretch of low ground to the meeting-place of the Harlem River and Spuyten Duyvil Creek, which separate Manhattan Island from the main-land. He who would know how the latter stream got its name will find the story set forth at length in the pages of Diedrich Knickerbocker. That truthful chronicle tells us that when Anthony Van Corlear, Governor Stuyvesant's trumpeter, was sent to rouse to war the country beyond the Harlem, he came to this stream to find no ferry-boat. His mission, however, did not brook delay, and though the water was turbulent and the wind high, he swore he would cross en spuyt den duyvel,—in spite of the devil,—and with a generous pull at his stone bottle he plunged into the stream. When a few yards from the shore, says Knickerbocker, "he was seen to struggle violently, and, giving a vehement blast of his trumpet, sank forever to the bottom. The clangor of the trumpet aroused the people far and near, who hurried to the spot in amazement. Here an old Dutch burger, famed for his veracity, and who had been a witness of the fact, related to them the melancholy affair, with the fearful addition (to which I am slow of giving belief) that he saw the devil, in the shape of a huge moss-bunker, seize the sturdy Anthony by the leg and drag him beneath the waves." And ever since the stream and the point at its mouth have been called Spuyten Duyvil.

"What gave this place so curious a name?" a young woman once asked a stranger by her side as the Hudson River train on which they were riding halted at Spuyten Duyvil Station. He told her the legend of Anthony the Trumpeter. "Poor fellow! did he leave a family?" was her sympathetic inquiry at the story's end. Her companion, with the delicacy of a modest man, referred her to Knickerbocker's chronicle, which tells us that "though he was never married, yet did he leave behind him some two or three dozen children in different parts of the country, fine, chubby, brawling, flatulent little urchins, from whom, if legends speak true (and they are not apt to lie), did descend the race of editors who people and defend the country, and who are bountifully paid by the people for keeping up a constant alarm and making them miserable."

Where the Harlem River and Spuyten Duyvil Creek mingle their waters, a small island, crossed by a foot-bridge, connects the Borough of Manhattan with the Borough of the Bronx. A few yards west of Goodwin's Island, as this strip of land is called, was "the wading-place" that in the day of first things afforded communication between the Island of Manhattan and the mainland; and thence a short walk carries one to the site of the ancient hamlet of Fordham, which nestled at the base of Tetard's Hill, on the east bank of the Harlem, near the Kingsbridge station of the New York and Putnam Railroad. John Archer, or Jan Arcer, as he signed his name, in 1671 became the owner of an estate that extended from Spuyten Duyvil Creek to the present High Bridge, and from the Harlem to the Bronx, borrowing from the little settlement which grew up beside the ford over Spuyten Duyvil Creek the name of the Manor of Fordham. There remains no trace of the original hamlet, but the present settlement of Fordham preserves the memory of the manor of which it once formed a part.

The wading-place was for a long time the only

means of communication between Manhattan and Westchester; but in 1669, by order of Governor Lovelace, a ferry and an inn were established between Goodwin's Island and the present Kingsbridge. One John Verveelen kept the ferry and inn for many years, and was succeeded by his son, who served as ferryman and landlord until the erection of the King's Bridge, which crosses Spuyten Duyvil Creek a few rods west of Goodwin's Island. The building of this bridge was proposed in 1692, and the same year the mayor and alderman of New York petitioned the governor: "That as Frederick Philipse will undertake to build the bridge at the said place, for the conveniency of all travellers and droves of cattle, at a moderate and reasonable toll, they do therefore humbly pray that if the said Philipse will undertake in one year's time, to build a good and convenient drawbridge, for the passage of all travellers, droves of cattle, and passage of carts and waggons, for the toll of one penny for every neat cattle, and two pence for each man and horse, and twelve pence for each score of hogs and sheep, and for each cart and waggon that shall pass thereon, that he may have the preference of their Majesties' grant for the same by having a bridge built there."

The following year the ferry and island were confirmed to Philipse by royal charter, and he was empowered to build and maintain a toll-bridge, which was to be twenty-four feet wide, free to all the king's forces, and was to be called the King's Bridge. It was built and opened before the end of 1693, and for the better part of a century its revenues added to the wealth of its owners. The Boston and Albany stages crossed the bridge in order to reach the mainland, and during the Revolution it played an important part in the movements of both armies, several engagements taking place in its vicinity. The earthworks thrown up by the British can still be traced on the adjacent hills, and only a few years ago the remains of a British officer were unearthed not a stone's throw from the bridge, with the number of his regiment still legible on the brass buttons of his uniform.

A little to the north of the King's Bridge stands an old, tree-girt house of stone, known in the locality as the Macomb mansion. The date of its erection is uncertain, but there is good ground for the belief that it was built before 1700 as an inn for travellers passing to and from Manhattan. Daniel Halsey was its host between 1789 and 1793, and six years later it became the property of Alexander Macomb, a merchant of New York, who in 1810 sold it to his son Robert. The latter afterwards expended a large sum of money in building a dam across the Harlem at what now is the foot of One Hundred and Fifty-fifth Street. Macomb's Dam was furnished with gates that opened to the flood-tide setting in from the East River and closed to the ebb-tide, thus converting the upper Harlem into a mill-pond. The dwellers along the lower shores of the river rebelled at the degradation to a muddy creek of the stream by their doors, and, coming up in a body, smashed the dam. Its name, however, still clings to the neighborhood, and for many years Macomb's Dam Bridge—a wooden structure now replaced by one of iron—has spanned the river at One Hundred and Fifty-fifth Street, connecting Harlem Heights with the annexed district. The wrecking of his dam bankrupted Macomb, and the tavern and the land around it passed into other hands. Long may the present owners of the ancient structure guard it from destruction.

Beyond Kingsbridge lie what were once the wide-spreading lands of the Philipse family, now in part included within the limits of the greater city. A veritable principality was the manor and lordship of Philipseburg. It extended from the Harlem to the Croton, and from the Bronx to the Hudson, with its manor-houses at Yonkers and Pocantico and its princely residence in the city; and at the time of the Revolution had been in the family over a hundred years. The Philipse of that day was Frederick, third lord of the manor, a refined and amiable man, but stubborn in his adherence to the cause of the crown. Washington ordered him removed from his Yonkers manor-house to New Rochelle and from there to Connecticut, where he was put on his parole not to go beyond the limits of Middletown. He obtained permission, however, to return to New York for a visit, and when recalled failed to respond. Then his estate was confiscated, and he fled to England, established himself at Chester, and, dying there in 1785, was buried in the cathedral, where a monument proclaims his virtues and lauds his loyalty to the king. No part of his lands remains in the possession of his descendants.

Philipseburg manor lives in history as the Neutral Ground over which during the Revolution cowboys and skinners—British and American bands of marauders—roved and plundered at will. Over this domain marched and counter-marched the Continental army; here rested the French troops under Rochambeau; and here the loyalists carried on a wanton and destructive warfare while the British held New York. An historic corner is this strip of land between the Harlem and the Bronx, with its every rood enriched with the blood of heroes or made memorable by deeds of daring and suffering. The way to it should never lack for pilgrims, for it leads to consecrated ground.

XV

Little Sisters of Manhattan

SIX in number are the smaller islands that cluster around Manhattan, and each holds for the pilgrim a story charged with varied and moving incident. That of Governor's Island, set down like a giant emerald on a woman's breast in the upper waters of the bay, has its beginning in the days when Wouter Van Twiller ruled New Amsterdam and directed its affairs with careful regard for his own advancement. The Indian name of this island was Pagganck, or Nut Island, lengthened by the Dutch into Noton, or Nutten Island, and when, in 1637, Van Twiller bought it from the Indian owners, giving them "in exchange an axe-head or two, a string of beads, and a few nails," the half-mile channel which now separates it from the Long Island shore was shallow enough to allow the fording of cattle.

Van Twiller held the island, which he used as a goat-pasture, for little more than a year. It reverted to the West India Company when his indifferently honest rule came to an end, and in

1639 was leased by "the honorable, wise, and right prudent Mr. William Kieft" to Evert Bischop, Sibout Claesen, and Harman Bastiansen, who "acknowledged to have amiably agreed and covenanted for the hire of it." They were to pay a yearly rent of five hundred merchantable pine and oak planks, and also bound themselves to keep in repair the saw-mill which had been built on the island at the company's expense, and to deliver it in as good order as they had received it.

We know not when the tenancy of Bischop and his fellows came to an end, but after Dutch had given place to English rule, Nutten Island, with its groves of oak, hickory, and chestnut, became in 1698 a perquisite attached to the office of governor of the province, and thenceforth takes its place in history as Governor's Island. Some of the governors leased the island for their own profit, and there has come down to us a quaint petition from one Richard Deane to Lord Dunmore in 1770 begging for a continuance of a two years' lease executed a few months before the latter assumed the governorship. Deane recites that he has been at great expense in cultivating the island, and that it has been the custom of former governors upon entering office to continue its tenant for the time he had taken it. "Therefore," he says, "your lordship's petitioner most humbly submits his hopes to your lordship's great goodness, not doubting to find that tender benevolence for which your lordship is so justly esteemed; and obtain your lordship's permission to continue and proceed on in his business. . . . Your lordship's petitioner has been led by the ruling hand of kind Providence to the honor of being your lordship's first tenant in America, in which situation he is determined to merit your lordship's attention by a direct adherence to every duty incumbent on him, which he humbly hopes will meet your lordship's approbation. And your petitioner, as in duty bound, will not only forever pray; but will pay your lordship's rent very punctually."

The promise with which Deane closed his petition no doubt made effective appeal to Lord Dunmore, and surely would have warmed the heart of an earlier English governor,—Lord Cornbury. That dubiously upright nobleman held possession of Governor's Island from 1702 until 1708, and was so impressed by its charms that when in the year first named the assembly voted fifteen hundred pounds to defend the Narrows against possible assault by the French, he applied the money, Colden tells us, "to building a pleasure-house thereon for himself and succeeding governors to retire to, when he inclined to free himself from business." Cornbury's high-handed proceeding brought him a sharp rebuke from the assembly, and, as we know, was one of the opening wedges in the breach between crown and colonies which led to the Revolution.

When the clash of arms finally came, and New York, after the capture of Boston, became the storm-centre of the conflict, the patriot forces hastened to possess and fortify Governor's Island. "Last evening," wrote Colonel Silliman, of Connecticut, to his wife, on April 9, 1776, "drafts were made from a number of regiments here, mine among the rest, to the amount of one thousand men. With these and a proper number of officers General Putnam at candle-lighting embarked on board of a number of vessels, with a large number of intrenching tools, and went directly on the island a little below the city, called Nutten Island, where they have been intrenching all night, and are now at work and have got a good breastwork there raised, which will cover them from the fire of the ships." The end of a fortnight found Prescott's men from Bunker Hill encamped behind these defences; later they were joined by the Fourth Continental Infantry; and early in August Washington, speaking through Lord Stirling, declared Governor's Island "better guarded than any other post of the army."

But after the battle of Long Island and the defeat of the Americans, Admiral Howe despatched four ships to attack the island, from which the garrison hastily retreated to the city, though without the loss of a man or a gun, whereupon the British took possession and further fortified and garrisoned it. The war ended and independence secured, the republican successor of the royal governors was confirmed by the legislature in one of their privileges, the use of Governor's Island; and in 1784 Governor George Clinton leased it for the purpose of a race-course and hotel. Races were run there in 1785 and 1786, but its career as a pleasure-resort, along with the tenure of the governor, came soon to an end. The legislature in 1790 voted the use of it to the regents of the University, for the benefit of Columbia College and the various academies under their rule, and it was forthwith leased to one John Price at an annual rental of ninety-three pounds.

The legislature, however, reserved the right to

claim part of the island, if it were needed for public defence, and in 1794 a renewed fear of invasion, this time by the French, caused it to again become a military post. Earnest demand was made at the same time that it should be more strongly fortified. The State of New York being in debt to the general government, Congress turned a deaf ear to this demand, but it agreed that any money expended by the State on its fortification should be credited against its debt. Under this arrangement, the legislature in 1794 appropriated thirty thousand pounds for fortifications at or near New York, and between that year and 1806 upward of a hundred and ten thousand dollars were devoted to works on Governor's Island. Fort Jay was built under the stress of the French "scare" of 1797, but was voted inadequate, and in 1806 replaced by Fort Columbus, an enclosed pentagonal work which fills the centre of the island and is surrounded by a moat. Five years later a circular granite battery called Castle William was built on a bed of rocks at the extreme westerly point of the island. Neither of these, once counted essential to the safety of New York, has ever been the target of a hostile shot, and both are now in a condition of crumbling decay.

Castle William, however, is something more than a picturesque relic of the past. During the Civil War more than a thousand Confederates were confined within its walls at one time, and it is still used as a prison for military offenders. One of the prisoners of the Civil War period was John Yates Beall, who in 1864 headed a daring plot to seize the federal gunboat "Michigan" and release some three thousand Confederate officers confined on Johnson's Island, Lake Erie. The first step in this plot was the capture of the "Philo Parsons," a small steamer which ran between Detroit and Sandusky, touching at Put-in-Bay and other islands. Three sons of John Brown, of Harper's Ferry fame, were then residents of Put-in-Bay, and were present when the captured vessel tied up at that island. It was in the hands of disguised Confederates, but the Browns became suspicious, and hastening to their home, so located as to be sheltered from observation at the landing-place, got into a row-boat, and put off for Johnson's Island, eight miles distant. Taking advantage of a heavy mist and bending to their oars with desperate energy, they reached the "Michigan" a quarter-hour ahead of the Confederates. The captain of the gunboat, thus forewarned, was able to foil the

NEW YORK FROM FORT COLUMBUS, GOVERNOR'S ISLAND, IN 1816

plot in its inception. Beall sank the "Philo Parsons" near the Canadian shore, and escaped with his men, but was captured after four months, convicted of piracy, and in 1865 hanged on the parade-ground at Fort Columbus.

Governor's Island was in 1800 ceded by the State of New York to the United States, and in 1821 Federal military head-quarters were transferred to it from the city. It was for many years following 1852 the principal depot of the recruiting service, and it has been since 1878 the headquarters of the Department of the Atlantic. The army post of Fort Columbus occupies the whole of the island except six acres on its northeastern shore given up to the New York Arsenal. An afternoon stroll about the island is a memory to keep for a lifetime. The view from the parapet of Castle William reaches far and wide over the river and the bay, while at one's feet lies the island, with its granite bastions, its low earthworks, its grassy moat, its arsenal, and its stretches of green lawn; and over all towers the flag-staff, with its tri-colored banner, once the token of a struggling cause, but now the emblem of a mighty power upon whose dominions the sun never sets.

Bedloe's Island, which takes its name from its

first recorded owner, Isaac Bedloe, a merchant of New Amsterdam, is known only to folk of these latter days as the site of the Statue of Liberty, but it, too, has played its part in history. Commanding the Narrows as it does, it was regarded as the chief point of defence for the city of New York at a time when wooden ships were all that could be arrayed against it. It was for that reason ceded to the general government, and a fort reared there in the opening years of the last century; but in 1839 orders went forth that this defence should be replaced by a fortification able to cope with the most powerful fleet of an enemy. The fort thus begun was in the form of a star surrounded by a moat, while outside of that, on the eastern and southern fronts of the island, was an earthwork, based on a granite wall. In each corner of the parapet surrounding the fort was an embrasure, from which an enfilading fire would sweep the moat to the point of the opposite wall, rendering impossible an assault by a scaling party, even should the outer works be carried. The forty-five guns which the works mounted could all be so trained as to plant every shot within the space of a barrel-head at any designated point in the Narrows.

Work on Fort Wood, as it was called, continued until the opening of the war with Mexico gave the engineers of the army work to do in other fields. A few years later came the era of iron ships and of long-range guns enabling a hostile fleet to shell New York without entering the harbor, and these changed conditions brought the dismantlement of the works upon which the city had relied as its chief defence in time of war. After that Bedloe's was an island without a history until in 1883 it furnished a site for the Statue of Liberty executed by Frederic Bartholdi and presented by France to the United States as a memorial to the friendly relations between the two nations dating from the Revolution.

Before the days of fort and statue Bedloe's Island was a well-known duelling-ground and the scene of at least one fatal encounter. Stephen Price in the opening decades of the last century was one of the wealthiest men in New York, a leader in society and in politics, and the manager of the Park Theatre. His brother during the Revolution had been provoked into a quarrel and killed by a Captain Nelson of the British army. Long afterwards, when others had forgotten the incident, Price learned by accident that Captain Nelson was visiting New York. Though ill from gout, he managed to hobble to the City Hotel and call on Nelson.

"You foully killed my brother, you murderer," was his greeting. "Shall I pull your nose and knock you down, or will you take the assurance as sufficient?"

"The assurance is enough, sir."

Seconds were chosen, and three days later they met on Bedloe's Island, where Nelson was shot through the heart at the first fire.

About the time that Wouter Van Twiller bought Governor's Island, he also became the owner, through sharp bargaining with the Indians, of what are now known as Blackwell's, Ward's, and Randall's Islands in the East River. The Indians called Blackwell's Minnahannonck, and the Dutch The Long Island, which name clung to it for half a hundred years. John Manning, who had begun life as captain of a coasting vessel, and later had been an officer in the colonial forces, was appointed sheriff of New York after its first conquest by the British, and from the emoluments of the office bought The Long Island, which, reverting to the West India Company upon the downfall of Van Twiller, had now become a part of the common lands of the colony. Hardly, however, had he built a house on his island retreat before his official career was brought to a sudden and hapless end. Governor Lovelace was absent from New York when, in August, 1673, a Dutch fleet entered the bay and demanded the surrender of the town, and Manning, who commanded the fort, yielded without firing a shot at the enemy.

It was said, and believed by many, that he had been bribed by the Dutch. When the British recovered the province in the following year he was tried by court-martial, found guilty of cowardice and treachery, and, though his influence at court saved him from the sentence of death, he was adjudged to have his sword broken over his head and to be forever debarred from holding any office in the gift of the crown. The former part of the sentence was carried out on a November day in 1674, in front of the old City Hall in Pearl Street, and Manning, with full purse, but a tarnished name, retired to his East River island, there to spend the remainder of his days. When he died the island passed to his daughter, whose husband, Robert Blackwell, gave it the name by which it has ever since been known. It remained in the possession of Blackwell's descendants until 1828, when it became the property of the city. Since then it has been occupied by the charity hospital, the penitentiary, the almshouse, the work-house, and the asylum for the pauper insane.

North of Blackwell's Island aforetime lay the rocks which made the narrow stretch of water called Hell Gate the dread of all mariners voyaging to and from the Sound. Two thousand vessels more or less completely wrecked in the rush and whirl of its waters was Hell Gate's sinister record, when in 1866 the general government began the removal of the rocks which so long had caused dismay to sailors. The work covered a period of nineteen years, demanding a high degree of engineering skill, but one by one the rocks yielded to the drill and to dyanmite until finally in 1885 a depth of twenty-six feet was attained throughout the length of Hell Gate. The name which the Dutch gave it, however, promises to cling to it through the long future, if only as a grim reminder of its earlier history.

What with its hills and dales, once covered with dense woodlands, time was when Ward's Island, on the hither side of Hell Gate, was one of the loveliest spots in America, and it is yet so beautiful as to compel the praise of all visitors. It was called Tenkenas when Wouter Van Twiller bought it from the Indian chiefs Heyseys and

Numers, and giving it the name of Great Barent's Island, converted its two hundred and forty acres into a pasturage for his cattle. It passed through various hands after Van Twiller's downfall, and following the British conquest of the province was granted with its neighbor Randall's Island to Thomas Delavall, who owned a farm at Harlem and found it useful for grazing purposes. After that it was known as Buchanan's Island, and was so called when, in September, 1776, Howe occupied it with British and Hessian troops and made use of it to keep in check the patriots at Harlem. Jasper and Bartholomew Ward became its owners in 1806 and gave it their name. Still later the city purchased seventy acres of the island for a potter's field, and there at the present time a silent host of tenscore thousand take their rest in unmarked graves. The corporation now owns all of Ward's Island, using it for hospital and asylum purposes.

Randall's Island, separated from its larger neighbor by Little Hell Gate, had a varied and stirring history before it passed into the hands of the man from whom it takes its present name. When Thomas Delavall, its first English owner, died in 1682 he left Little Barent's Island, as it was then called, to his daughter, who had married James Carteret, one of the lord proprietors of New Jersey. Carteret's daughter became the wife of Philip Pipon, of the Island of Jersey, whose two sons agreed after his death to share the family property by the older one taking all the estate that lay in England and the younger all that lay in America. Under this arrangement Elias Pipon came hither with his family in 1732, and erected a house on Little Barent's Island, to which, moved by its beauty and romantic situation, he gave the name of Belle Isle. Pipon's mode of living, however, was not in keeping with his purse. He was compelled within a twelvemonth to borrow money on his estate, and at the end of five years had to make an assignment for the benefit of his creditors.

Thus Belle Isle found a new owner in one St. George Talbot, whom the records describe "as an amiable English gentleman with an eye to the romantic," and who made his home on the island, then called Talbot's Island, until his death. That event befell in 1765, and seven years later Talbot's executors sold the island to John Montresor, a British captain of engineers, then stationed in New York, who gave it his name and made it his home until the end of the Revolution.

During that struggle, however, Montresor's Island was also occupied by British troops, and was once attacked by the patriot forces. The British had placed a quantity of stores and ammunition on the island, and the Americans determined to seize them. On the night of September 24, 1776, a week after the battle of Harlem Heights, a body of two hundred and fifty picked men, led by Major Thomas Henley, of Massachusetts, descended upon the island, and their well-laid plans for its capture would have succeeded had not an impetuous soldier given warning to the British garrison by the premature discharge of his gun. The Americans, nevertheless, charged the enemy's works, defended by twice their numbers, but in the end were repulsed with heavy loss. Among the killed was Major Henley, one of the most promising of officers, who fell at the head of his men. His comrades recovered his body, carried it back to camp, and buried it beside that of Colonel Thomas Knowlton, who the week before had met an equally heroic fate on Harlem Heights.

Captain Montresor left America at the time of the evacuation of New York by the British, and in 1783 he sent from Kent in England a letter to a friend enclosing two powers of attorney, " one to dispose of my desolate island," and " the other of everything I possess within those distracted discoveries of Master Kit Columbus." Thus in 1784 Montresor's Island became the property of Samuel Ogden, who sold it before the year's end to Jonathan Randel, a young farmer of Harlem. Randel agreed to give twelve thousand dollars for it, and cultivated its soil to such good purpose that he was able within ten years to pay the whole of this sum. It was from his executors that the city in 1835 bought the island, which perpetuates his memory, though popular usage has worked a change in the manner of spelling his name. It now affords a site for the House of Refuge for juvenile delinquents.

City Island, at the head of the Sound, was once a part of Westchester County, but since 1895 has been included within the corporate limits of the city. It was in 1654 that Thomas Pell bought from the Indians a tract of land which included what afterwards became the towns of Westchester, Pelham, and New Rochelle, along with what was then known as Minneford's Island. John Pell, second lord of the manor established by his uncle, sold this island in 1685 to one John Smith, and after passing through sundry hands it became in 1781 the property of

Joseph Palmer, of Throg's Neck, who soon after conveyed it to his brother Benjamin. Then it was that it earned the name of City Island and a place in history, for its owner was a man given to dreams, and the dream which most held his thought was the founding of a city on his island domain which should rival New York. Hell Gate made the passage from the Sound into the waters of New York harbor a perilous one, and Palmer argued that any plan by which it could be avoided would be hailed with enthusiasm. Minneford's Island seemed to him to offer an admirable solution of the problem. It was a central point in the highway of commerce, there were natural harbors and protection from storms, and land for dwelling-houses and stores.

Palmer accordingly set to work with energy and considerable shrewdness to give shape and substance to his dream. A bridge was projected from the island to the main-land; the former was plotted and a city plan prepared which provided slips and dock for ships of all sizes; and advertisements were published setting forth the good fortune that would accrue to all who shared in the enterprise. And for the moment all went well. Many of the lots in the future city sold for ten pounds each, and Palmer was offered three hundred and a thousand pounds for different portions of his land. But then came the Revolution, and with it the capture of the island by the British. Palmer himself was taken prisoner, and though he was allowed after a time to go with his family to New York, where he remained until the end of the war, it was upon conditions which later led to the seizure of his property. He petitioned in vain for its return, and in helpless age was only saved from want by the generous aid of Aaron Burr and a few other friends. And such was the sorry ending of his dream of a water-girt city. Seventy years after his death, however, the bridge he had hoped to build was opened to the public, while now trade has sprung up on his island, and all about it is heard the hum of enterprise.

Pelham Point, opposite City Island, recalls one of the least known but for the patriots most brilliant actions of the Revolution. After the battle of Harlem Heights, in the autumn of 1776, Washington began withdrawing his army to the Westchester hills, but owing to lack of proper facilities his progress was necessarily slow and his force much exposed, offering to a vigilant enemy an excellent opportunity for attack. Howe, noting these facts, determined if possible to get to the rear of Washington, force him to retreat to the Harlem, and there catch him between two fires. With this purpose in mind, he landed at Pelham Point on October 18, 1776, and began to march towards Pelham Manor, but only to find his progress disputed by the sailors and fisherfolk, commanded by Colonel John Glover, who had done such good service during the retreat from Long Island. The patriot force numbered less than eight hundred men, and with it Glover was to check the advance of some four thousand British and Hessian regulars long enough to enable Washington to safely reach White Plains.

A desperate and seemingly hopeless task, but Glover proved equal to it, repeating on the plains of Westchester the story of Bunker Hill. He disposed his little band with masterly skill, tempting the enemy with a small force, then retreating and luring them to a point where they offered a target to two hundred Continentals hidden behind a stone wall. The fight that followed inflicted terrific punishment upon the British and Hessians. Eight hundred of them were killed or wounded,—a loss equal to the number of Americans engaged in the affair,—and Howe's advance was checked long enough for Washington to complete his retreat to White Plains. Indeed, the battle of Pelham Point, dismissed by most historians with a line or two, was one of those drawn encounters that mean more than victory. It not only saved the patriot army, but fired it with new hope. Washington issued a congratulatory address to Glover and his men, and never had they in after-days opportunity for weightier service to their country.

The region about Pelham Point also has intimate association with a woman, whose stormy life and tragic end make her one of the winningly pathetic figures of the colonial period. Ann Marbury was the daughter of a Puritan minister, whose home was near old Boston in England. There she spent her girlhood and became the wife of William Hutchinson, with whom in 1634 she came to the new Boston on this side of the sea. A beautiful woman and a generous-minded and highly gifted one as well, the story of the part she played in the affairs of the infant town is a familiar one. It led, as we know, to her banishment, first to Rhode Island, where her husband died, and then to Flushing, whence with her fatherless children and a few devoted followers she crossed to and found a refuge on the Westchester shore. She had her house built on the rising ground near Pelham Point, and her life in the wilderness promised to be a peaceful and happy one. It was a delusive promise. The savage Indian wars of Kieft's time had already begun, and the red men in their reprisals spared not the innocent and the helpless. On a September night in 1643 a party of them surrounded the Hutchinson cabin and fired it from several sides. When the frightened woman tried to rush out she was driven back to die in the flames. Her eldest son, a lad of twelve, escaped only to be burned at the stake; while the little sister, whom he had carried from the house, was taken by the Indians and lived among them so long that she was unwilling to return with the white men who effected her rescue in after years. The site of Ann Hutchinson's house is as yet unmarked, but it was definitely located a short time ago, and a movement is under way to place a suitable tablet on the spot.

Pilgrimage to it ends these rambles through and around old New York. And they have been well worth the taking, for though at times they have followed oft-travelled and familiar pathways, they have also led to many a neglected nook and corner, and at a hundred turns have proved how rich in human interest and in moving and heroic incident is the history of the city which in a present of noble and widening achievement faces a future that will make it the glory and the wonder of the world.

INDEX

C

D

E

N

Q

R

S

END OF VOL. II

www.ingramcontent.com/pod-product-compliance
Lightning Source LLC
LaVergne TN
LVHW020559110826
845149LV00002B/315

* 9 7 8 1 4 1 8 1 8 8 3 0 6 *